# The **VWBUS**

## History of a Passion

Responsible for contents: Jörg Hajt
Editors:
 Martin Henze
 Jürgen Schlegelmilch
Cover photo: Andreas Beyer
Setup and formation: Ralf Kolmsee, F5
 Mediengestaltung, Königswinter

Originally published in German as *VW BUS, Geschichte einer Leidenschaft* in 2011 by HEEL Verlag GmbH
Translated by Dr. Edward Force

Copyright © 2012 by Schiffer Publishing, Ltd.
Translation by Ed Force

Library of Congress Control Number: 2012937491

Cover design by Bruce Waters

Type set in Zurich BT

ISBN: 978-0-7643-4074-1
Printed in China

Published by Schiffer Publishing, Ltd.
4880 Lower Valley Road
Atglen, PA 19310
Phone: (610) 593-1777; Fax: (610) 593-2002
E-mail: Info@schifferbooks.com
Web: www.schifferbooks.com

For our complete selection of fine books on this and related subjects, please visit our website at www.schifferbooks.com. You may also write for a free catalog.

Schiffer Publishing's titles are available at special discounts for bulk purchases for sales promotions or premiums. Special editions, including personalized covers, corporate imprints, and excerpts, can be created in large quantities for special needs. For more information, contact the publisher.

We are always looking for people to write books on new and related subjects. If you have an idea for a book, please contact us at proposals@schifferbooks.com.

# The
# VWBUS
## History of a Passion

Jörg Hajt

4880 Lower Valley Road • Atglen, PA 19310

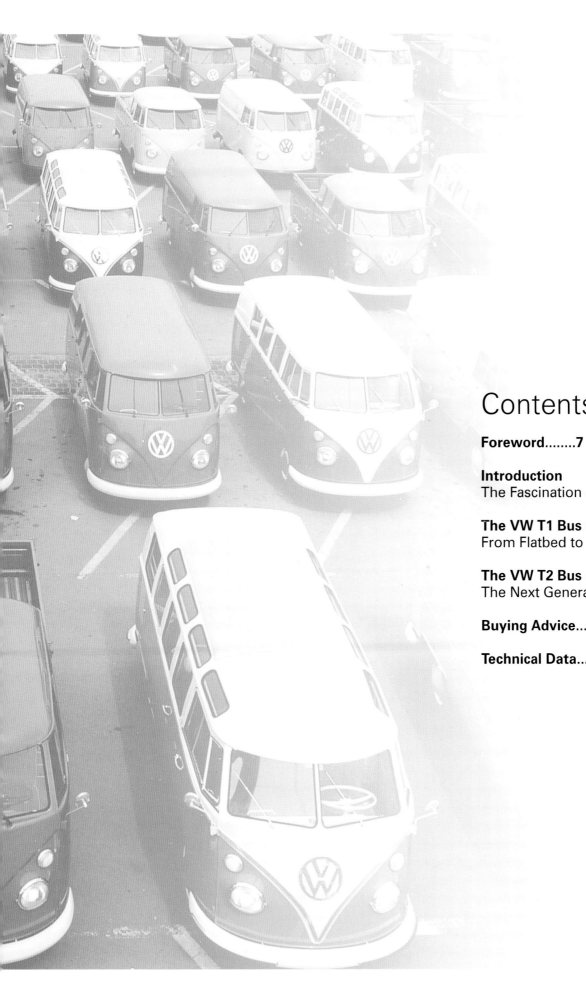

# Contents

# Foreword

In November 1949, a new epoch in automotive history began with the introduction of the first small transporter by Volkswagen. Like no other light utility vehicle before, the stubby space-saver from Wolfsburg, only 4150 mm long, influenced the development of a completely new generation of universally useful minibuses. The Beetle derivative, available as a box van, small bus, or flatbed truck, known as Type 2 at the factory, went beyond that to achieve a noteworthy contribution to the motorizing of countless service and artisan businesses, becoming, not without reason, one of the most style-setting symbols of the "German Economic Miracle."

Now, six decades after its debut, the "Bulli," as the Volkswagen Transporter has been lovingly named by its legion of fans, has lost none of its fascination, and thus the classic rear-engined vehicles enjoy a steadily growing popularity and increased value.

Besides a compact historical outline of the vehicle's history, the intention of this book is to offer a photographic overview of the subjectively most beautiful or technically most interesting T1 and T2 models that remain. The author extends his thanks to all the institutions and Volkswagen fans who have contributed to the existence of this book by making information or photographic material available. Hearty thanks are also extended to all who have made their vehicles available for photographing.

Jörg Hajt

Wattenscheid, March 2011

# The Fascination of the VW Bus

Countless antique car fans have already thought about why the VW Bus has inspired such a great fascination, while its contemporaries now exist in the shadows of public awareness. A decisive answer is not easy to formulate at this point, and so we can only speculate as to why the Bulli, along with the Beetle, could rise to become a international favorites.

For one thing, the classless charm of the VW Transporter plays a major role. As a Samba Bus or in a luxury version, it was just as practical as a classy travel vehicle as it was as a blue-collar dumper at building sites or a combined family car and small van for commercial gardens or at weekly markets. In automotive history the Bulli thus had an almost revolutionary impact. Successful business people and show-business stars drove it over the world's roads with just as much pleasure as the everyday driver in his daily trip to the office or factory. A veteran auto journalist once said of the Beetle that it had democratized auto driving. Without qualification, the same evaluation is true for the VW Transporter.

For another, to this day the T1 and T2 possess all the same German virtues that justify its utilitarian and long-term investment. The VW Transporter is practical and slick at the same time. Its form is timeless and impressive. Often one detail of the vehicle stands out to make it noticed among the masses of automobiles. Its reliability is proverbial, and ordinary people have made it a more lovable than perfect means of travel for a lifetime. Its functionality, even after more than half a century, lacks nothing compared with newer vehicles, and its close relationship to the Beetle also attracts unenvious glances from neighbors, even though its market value has long since pushed its way into the price ranges of modern upper-class sedans. Then too, its appearance changed but little between 1949 and 1979, which not only provides a high recognition value but also suggests stability in the often very hectic life of the automobile. Whereas, for example, a venerable Ford Transit, whether as a front-engine or a long-hood truck, can be recognized as such only by the practiced eye, the T1 and T2 do not puzzle even the automotive layman. Their once-widespread use as postal, municipal, and commercial vehicles also awakens memories of one's childhood or youth, when a longingly awaited parcel from a great aunt arrived with a yellow VW Transporter model, or the ice man appeared in the neighborhood punctually at 3:00 P.M. in summer with his high-roof bus rebuilt into a delivery van. For lack of one's own driveable vehicle, it was often enough the boss's VW Transporter in which the new holder of a driver's license was allowed to make the first drive through his home town. And in intellectual circles as well, the Bulli has held cult status, at least since 1968. For semester break, one set out in a glaringly painted VW Bus with an equally colorful gang of like-minded colleagues on an awareness-enlarging tour to the Bosporus, where the chassis not only had to show its enormous suspension comfort on unpaved roads, to say nothing of the legendary hippie trails that led the bus and passengers to Afghanistan, India, or the American Wild West. Perhaps with the exception of the Citroen 2 CV, the Bulli incorporated "peace and happiness" in pure culture like no other vehicle. It is no wonder that both the T1 and T2 made an impression on people's minds. Like the Beetle, the VW Transporter is also almost overloaded with personal memories, and its driver is often the recipient of a nostalgic need to relate them. The repertoire runs from "My father drove the same bus" to detailed accounts from family or business life, in which now and then a yellowed black-and-white photo is taken out of one's wallet and proudly shown to one's listeners beside the family's new VW Bus or when unloading any kind of cargo.

But even those who have never owned a VW Bus themselves remember a remarkable lot about the qualities of the VW Transporter – whether the unmistakable sound of the boxer engine, the high degree of suspension comfort, or the thermal problems of traveling with a full load on a hot day. All of this keeps the mythology of the VW Bus alive to this day and contributes decisively to the fascination felt by generations who first saw the light of day much later than it did. For years the bus hobby has extended over the generations and turned the legions of fans into a worldwide family.

Since the T1 already had given way to its successor in 1967, it is long gone from the utility-vehicle scene. To be sure, at the beginning of the 1980s a few of them were still being used by volunteer fire companies or in municipal motor pools, but at this time great numbers of the remaining vehicles led a life as suppliers of spare parts or as garden gazebos. The sad majority had already ended their days in the scrap-metal converters of the steel industry. Comparatively few owners were at all aware of the historical value of the Wolfsburg best-seller. How could they, one might ask, when dozens of these vehicles were seen on the street every day?

Many buses and caravans had a far better life than these beasts of burden. Kept in much better condition, they were slowly made ready for a second life as a "young-timer." Well-kept T1s were available for the proverbial hearty handshake, since many owners did not want simply to turn them over to the scrap yard. Who would then have thought that a Samba Bus or a Westfalia camper would some day have the same value as a new Mercedes E-Class? In the end, the Transporter was still seen as a utility vehicle, and its new owner, working even harder to earn a living, was looked upon with suspicion as something of an oddity.

Thus it is no surprise that the introduction of the T2 into its new future as an automotive classic was much more difficult. To be sure, since its debut in 1967 it was unchallenged as it led the phalanx of light transporters and passenger buses, yet the aura of specialty never gripped it. While the T1 could still be recognized at a glance as a Beetle derivative and thus awakened a sort of nostalgia, the T2 simply looked too modern to be a potential oldie. It was also a victim of the mobile society that it had advanced. As a reasonably priced utility vehicle, it served in its old age as a courier or transport vehicle for countless one-man businesses. It was available for the most part from the roadside for little cash and kept alive with even less money. In view of its more modern successor, the T3, which united the advantages of the T2 with new technology of the then-current VAG, only few T2 drivers could accept the idea of not wanting to trade in their vehicle for the new model.

Whether as an admired exhibit in the VW Auto Museum in Wolfsburg, a well-kept former volunteer firefighters' vehicle, a team transporter in the historical auto racing scene, or an accurate replica of that extraordinary racing transporter with its wheelbase lengthened by 1.20 meters and used by the private Bunker Racing Team in America to carry a Porsche 550 Spyder in the mid-1950s and then displayed at the Techno Classica Show in 2007 – all body types of the VW Bus enjoy cult status today. *Photos: Volkswagen Auto Museum Foundation (1), Jürgen Schlegelmilch*

Thus most T2s were either traded-in hastily or driven to the bitter end, leading directly to waste disposal. Covered trucks and double-cabin types, in particular, were kept in use "to the last drop of oil," which has made these varieties the most sought-after rarities today. Then, too, the time was not yet ripe for the use of special vehicles, such as vendors' vans or refrigerator trucks, so that thousands of them also had to go the way of scrap iron. One fortunate exception, though, was the camper. More for practical reasons of acquiring a full-value caravan for a comparatively low price, a remarkable lot of campers have survived to the present. Many Bulli fans first found their way to the rear-engine bus as a camper, and thus their first

too small because of marriage or children. The tremendous available space was also the decisive factor for many buyers with no loyalty to the brand. This, of course, resulted in the fact that people with little technical knowledge of the VW bus turned to it, which thus instituted the commercialization of the formerly limited Bulli interest. Not only did spare-part prices go up steadily, so did the prices of the vehicles themselves. While a well-kept Samba Bus could be had for about 10,000 DM (US $5300) at the turn of the century, just ten years later the same amount in Euros (US $14,335) had to be paid. On the threshold of the third millennium at the latest, the T1 and T2 had reached classic prices. The postal service and army had long since auctioned off their

After 50 years this T1 still serves its original purpose as a carrier of merchandise for sale, as seen here at the annual Classic Days at Dyck Castle near Moenchengladbach. *Photo: Jürgen Schlegelmilch*

camper formed the foundation of a fine Transporter collection today.

The growing interest in the T1 and T2 led to the founding of numerous clubs and interest groups. Finally, Transporter drivers were no longer on their own when they had technical questions or needed rare spare parts. Beyond that, the Bus developed more and more into a second car for many Beetle fans, for whom the space in their Beetle had become

last T2 vehicles, so that now it took some luck to find one or another factory or volunteer fire company that offered a good buy. Well maintained and often with fewer than 10,000 km on their odometer, the red vehicles offered a solid entry into the world of Transporters. Many of the vehicles depicted in this book no longer show that their first career was as a fire truck; others, though, proudly display their origin.

This T1 box van of 1964 visits selected events. The former owner, a businessman from Bremen, customized the Bulli with a roof rack and a functioning awning. In the background is the Westfalia caravan trailer that originally went with it. *Photo: Jürgen Schlegelmilch*

After the municipal vehicle garages and firehouses were emptied, ambitious bus fans could only go outside Germany. Besides their West European neighbors, where, with the exception of Belgium and the Netherlands, the Bulli fever had not grown so strong, the USA became the promised land for the collector. An expedition over the big ditch was worthwhile, especially for the Westfalia camper that was so popular overseas, as shown by one or another vehicle depicted here.

The vehicles shown here are not always completely original. Many an ambulance was turned into a camping bus, and many Kombis used as construction or service trucks were rebuilt as personal buses. Even though these vehicles are not always completely authentic, they still give an undeniable overview of the Bulli history of more than sixty years. But there are also "purists" among Bulli owners who have kept their vehicle as completely original as possible and, with great love for details, question the slightest added part as to its vehicle-specific correctness. Besides the T1 camper, it is mainly the former T1 and T2 utility trucks and special models that are given the greatest attention in this realm. There are also a great many Transporters kept in unrestored original condition, including the T1 Cherry Picker or the T1 Clinomobil depicted in this book. These vehicles, with their natural patina, exude the charm of being special, and are impressive examples of the proverbial long life of the VW Transporter.

The following pictures of perfectly maintained examples of the Transporter illustrate the histories of the T1 and T2. They are the subjectively most beautiful or the technically most interesting examples of these series. While this can offer only a comparatively small selection of the vehicles that really deserve to be shown, it is a representative selection of the enormous spectrum of classic VW Transporters.

# The VW T1 Bus (1950-1967)

## FROM FLATBED TO CULT OBJECT

## The VW T1 Bus (1950-1967)
# FROM FLATBED TO CULT OBJECT

For the manifold transporting tasks involved in rebuilding war torn Europe, there was a tremendous need for light utility vehicles in Germany and its neighboring countries from 1945 on. In particular, the growing service industry urgently needed compact and economical transporters, since on the one hand, the delivery trucks built before 1939 were too weak or not usable, and on the other, the purchase of larger utility vehicles like the Opel Blitz or Mercedes L 701 was usually impossible because of their high prices.

a material transporter, based on the Kübelwagen, used at the factory and simply called "Flatbed" by the workers.

As part of a works meeting on April 23, 1947, for Colonel Charles Radclyffe of the British "Trade and Industry Division," who was responsible for the Allied oversight of the Volkswagen Works, Pon sketched for the first time the outlines of the small transporter that he envisioned: closed box body, cab-over steering, cargo space with access through a side door, 750 kg payload, and

The so-called flatbed truck, based on the chassis of the Kübelwagen, which was used at the VW factory to transport materials, inspired Benedict Pon with the idea of a multiuse transporter. *Photo: Volkswagen Auto Museum Foundation*

Faced with this panorama, Benedict Pon, later a Volkswagen importer in the Netherlands, developed the plan to build a utility vehicle based on the Beetle during a visit to the Volkswagen Works in Wolfsburg in 1947. He was inspired by

an air-cooled Beetle engine at the rear. While the commission chief of the Volkswagen Works, Major Ivan Hirst, was in favor of the project without reservations, Radclyffe rejected it with a reference to the lack of production capacity.

In early 1948, Heinrich Nordhoff, the former manager of the Opel Blitz factory in Brandenburg, was named as the new general manager of the Volkswagen Works. In the autumn of 1948, Nordhoff authorized the development of a box van based on Pon's concept. The design team, under the new Volkswagen development chief, Dr. Alfred Haesner, then designed two basic models, one with a flat and one with a round front. Nordhoff chose the presumably more aerodynamically favorable rounded variety, but in the first wind-tunnel tests of scale models it showed an air resistance value of 0.75 and could not fulfill the hopes placed on it. A new, more favorably streamlined design improved the score to a resistance value of 0.45, notable for that time. In comparison, a T3 developed 30 years later gave a Cw value of 0.44!

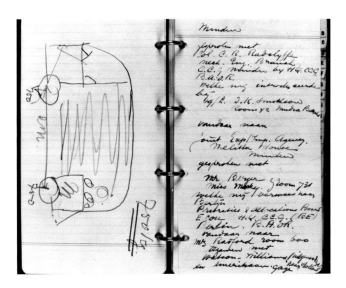

Above, on a visit to the factory early in 1947, Ben Pon drew the first sketches of his conception in his notebook. Below: The display of the first prototype took place in 1949. Test Vehicle No. 4 already showed the characteristic body elements of the later VW Type 29 delivery van, even though many details like door handles, rain gutters, and lighting had to be changed before production began in March 1950. *Photos: Volkswagen Auto Museum Foundation*

The first prototype of the factory's Type 29 special design for the box van was ready to drive on March 11, 1949. As it turned out, the Beetle chassis, favored by the works for reasons of cost and fitted with an auxiliary frame, proved to be fully overstressed after a few hundred kilometers in the road tests, which were carried out only at night. A second prototype, with a self-supporting body, strengthened Beetle front axle and experimental portal rear axle from the Type 82 (Kübelwagen), attained the torsion stiffness required for a utilitarian vehicle. But it was not only the body and chassis that caused problems. The engine gave more trouble than expected with the much higher vehicle weight. Porsche KG, under contract for the further development of the drive train, modified the gear transition for better acceleration and pulling power, though the top speed had to be reduced to 80 kph. Another "aerodynamically curved model" was hastily authorized for public road traffic, and finally, with Test Carrier No. 4, not only were the technically modified components tested satisfactorily, but the characteristic body shape for the T1 was accepted.

In the late summer of 1949, the factory management ordered four test vehicles, so they could begin marketing the new series by the year's end. Since it was still too soon for assembly-line construction, the four different looking prototypes were built by hand in less than three months. Unlike Pon's original sketch, only two of them had a windowless cargo area, while the other two prototypes had side windows to the rear.

At the official press showing on November 12, 1949, the two closed versions made their debut as "delivery vans for commerce and trade" or, in a version fitted with drawers, as "flying business vans." The vehicles with side windows were introduced by the marketing experts at Wolfsburg as "Kombiwagen" (with removable bench seats) or as "small buses for group trips." In their self-printed sales brochure, further variations were shown, including an ambulance, a milk truck, a parcel van, and radio and factory vans. Only a canvas-covered truck was missing, because Volkswagen was of the opinion that customers in that part of the market would prefer the heavier trucks made by their competitors.

The Allied forces also treasured the VW Transporter as being both reliable and economical. The photo shows a T1 pickup truck of the US Air Police during a fueling operation at the Berlin-Tegel airfield, circa 1955. *Photo: Schmidt Collection*

The introduction of the new Volkswagen Transporter took place at the time when Germany was divided. After the Federal Republic of Germany had come into being when the Basic Law took effect in the western zones on May 24, 1949, the German Democratic Republic arose on October 7 of the same year in the Soviet Occupation Zone. In the Petersburg Agreement of November 22, 1949, the first German Federal Chancellor, Konrad Adenauer, accomplished a revision of the occupation status. Certain limitations in the building of ocean ships were then lifted and the partial or complete halt of dismantling of numerous mines and factories in the Ruhr area, the Rhineland, and West Berlin took effect. In this way the economy of the young Federal Republic experienced a considerable rise, which worked out particularly positively for the domestic buying power and thus for the sale of the T1.

On March 8, 1950, mass production of the first VW box van began at the Volkswagen Works in Wolfsburg, with three models built at first. Unlike the Beetle, the Transporter's body had been designed as self-bearing. With a length of 4150 mm and a width of 1660 mm, the small Transporter, now officially named "Volkswagen Transporter Type 2," was only marginally larger than the Beetle, now called Type 1. The roof, 1900 mm high, was deliberately made capable of taking a roof rack and, along with the 2400 mm wheelbase, afforded a loading volume of 4.59 square meters, quite large for that class of vehicles. As already sketched by Pon, the load limit was 750 kg with an empty weight of 975 kg. Limited by the rear-engine concept, though, no full-length loading surface was possible, which is why a rear door was also excluded at first. The same applied to the rear window, in place of which a large VW logo appeared until November 1950. The new space-saver showed itself to be comparatively stingy. In the first model year it lacked a rear view, as well as a standard rear bumper until December 1953. In addition, all the windows were made flat to save costs, resulting not only in modest stability, but also in strong wind noise.

Under the floor at the rear was the four-cylinder boxer engine known from the Beetle, producing 25 HP and a displacement of 1131 cc. The running gear consisted of a double-crank link front axle with two torsion springs, one above the other, and the well-known swing rear axle with gearing (called a "portal axle"). The gearbox was also borrowed from the Beetle as modified by Porsche, with a modified ratio for second gear and the differential built into the opposite side. Thus the half-axles turned in the swing-axle tubes in the opposite direction to those on the Beetle. In the two side gear housings, two gears each converted the turning movement into driving power. On both axles there were the hydraulic drum brakes known

from the Beetle, and the somewhat indirect spindle linkage was also largely the same as that of the Wolfsburg Beetle.

The selling price of the VW Transporter, at first available only in pigeon blue or undercoat, was a proud 5850 DM (US $1400) at first, exactly 150 DM (about US $45) more than that of the fully equipped Beetle. In today's currency equivalent, this amounts to a price of some 14,500 Euros (US $18,700). What sounds like a bargain in today's terms was a real luxury at the time, as the average income in 1950 was just 279 DM (US $60) per month! Thus the T1 was seen only at larger businesses or in town or state service.

Production at the Hannover works in July 1957. Because of the large demand, the complete Transporter assembly had been moved from Wolfsburg to the new assembly halls in the previous year. *Photo: Volkswagen Auto Museum Foundation*

Only in 1958 did the double-cabin truck go into production at the Hannover works. Until then the Binz firm was under contract to produce the bodies. The double cab offered space for up to six people, but the rear seat could be entered only from the right. The side walls and tailgate could all be lowered. *Photo: Volkswagen Auto Museum Foundation*

In March 1950 there came the two-, five- and seven-seat Kombis, and an eight-seat minibus. At the same time, the first improvements were added to the regular production. The box van, like the personnel transporters, was offered with a two-stream heater in the cab and, as of September 1950, the bus could be had with rear interior heating. In addition, a bulkhead between the cab and cargo space made sure that passengers up front would not be hit by flying freight.

In 1951, the T1 took the lead in the sales of transporters and delivery vans in the Federal Republic. About a third of all new licenses in this category were granted to the Wolfsburg "Bulli," as it was popularly known. In view of this rapid success, the array of models was enlarged steadily. At the 1951 IAA Volkswagen introduced the "Small Bus Special Edition"—better known as the "Samba-Bus"—an especially luxurious eight-seater with panoramic windows, sun roof, and two-tone paint. The Westfalia firm of Wiedenbrück also produced the first T1-based

caravan, with its removable "Camping-Box," and the VW Transporter now became interesting for adventurers and globetrotters.

For a higher price, a sliding roof for the eight-seater was available as of June 1951. In December 1951, a largely standardized ambulance extended the array of special vehicles. While the patient had to be loaded laboriously through the double side doors of the box van rebuilt into an ambulance by the Miesen firm in Bonn, the Works model already had a wide-opening rear hatch, for which not only the engine housing had to be made smaller, but the fuel tank and spare wheel had to be moved. Since this rebuilding also allowed the designing of an open rear bed, a canvas-covered truck also became possible in the near future. To be sure, the parties responsible for the original T1 had decided against an open rear bed, but more and more voices of potential customers who no longer wanted to invest in a competitor's heavier model were heard.

On August 25, 1952, their wish was granted; the first flatbed VW Transporter, called the "Pritschenwagen," left the Wolfsburg works, gaining much attention from the automotive press. Its steel bed, measuring 2600 by 1570 mm, had a standard ramp height of barely a meter, so that it could be used to transport normal rolling goods. In addition to the rear bed, it had an enclosed cargo space of 1.90 cubic meters, the so-called "treasure chamber." With a base price of 6100 DM (US $1452), this truck was the lowest-priced VW transporter.

The price range of the closed version now ran from 6400 DM ($1500) for the box van to 9250 DM ($2200) for the Samba Bus. Despite this considerable increase of the base price, production increased to 21,665 units in 1952. But in the same year the Volkswagen GmbH had to deal with a bitter loss. It lost its development chief, Dr. Haesner, one of the fathers of the VW Transporter, who gave up his post to take one at Ford of Cologne. There he developed the FK 1000 box van, one of the T1's strongest competitors.

The derivative of the Ford Taunus 12 M, introduced in 1953, not only resembled the T1 visually, but was also, like it, a roomy cab-over type. With 38 HP from 1.2-liters of displacement, it seemed clearly more agile than the Type 2, so that it became a real rival in the rescue and minibus genres. Auto Union also increased its efforts to make its DKW F 89 L quick-loader a serious competitor. The Ingolstadt truck, available as a box van, minibus, kombi, pick-up, low-loader covered truck and vendor's van, was powered as of 1954 by a 30 HP, two-stroke engine, which allowed performance and loads comparable to those of the T1. The third of the German-made competitors was the Goliath Express, built from 1953 on; it was the first newly developed four-wheel delivery truck of the Borgward firm. As standard equipment of the top-line "Express Luxury Bus," with up to ten seats, it had, among others, panoramic windows, stressed-cloth side panels, and a sliding Golde roof 1440 mm long. With all this, the front-drive bus, with up to 40 HP, was not only aimed directly at the Samba Bus, but clearly undersold it with an original list price of 8070 DM ($1900). For a long time, though, the toughest competitor for dominance on the German small transporter market was the Vidal & Son Tempo Works with their Matador model. Interestingly, this light transporter, produced since 1949, also was powered by a Beetle engine until 1952, when VW General Manager Nordhoff had delivery to the competing firm halted. Optional two- or four-stroke engines from the Müller Design Bureau in Andernach were then installed, until Austin engines from Britain were finally obtained in 1957.

With a base price of 6100 Marksn (US $1452), the Pritschenwagen, especially popular with artisans, was the most reasonably priced VW Transporter. The first was completed at Wolfsburg in the summer of 1952. This photo shows its manufacture at the Hannover works in July 1957. *Photo: Volkswagen Auto Museum Foundation*

Yet the T1 remained best in its class, so that in 1953 the offerings were increased with a 10-meter "DL 10 Turning Ladder" truck made by the Meyer firm of Hagen, and a six-seat double-cab with a short flatbed made by the Binz firm of Lorch. In addition, the price list included the Westfalia "Camping Wagon" and the standardized "TSF-T Firefighting Vehicle" by Magirus, two other special versions made by outside suppliers since 1952.

Despite the continuing success, Volkswagen could not rest on its laurels. To compete with the main competitor, the Ford FK 1000, synchronized gearboxes (without first gear) were announced in the spring of 1953, heading a series of further improvements. A hydraulic telescopic steering damper not only made steering easier, but also prevented chassis bumps getting through to the steering wheel unfiltered. The performance of the generator was also raised to 160 watts, and the front doors of the cab were fitted with shaped adjustable vent windows for better cab ventilation.

Beyond that, the box van, kombi, and bus gained standard rear bumpers by the year's end.

In 1953, the daily production rose for the first time over the magic boundary of 100 vehicles. Thus the T1 had finally developed into a second, full-valued leg for the Volkswagen GmbH to stand on. To be able to have an impact on the small car and truck market overseas, Volkswagen opened the San Bernardo do Campo works in Brazil, its first production plant outside Germany. A year later it opened a second assembly plant in Australia. Under the new VW importer in the USA, Arthur Stanton, the Unites States grew to become an important sales market, so that the success story of the T1 grew from one high point to the next. After a stronger engine, producing 30 HP with a displacement of 1192 cc, had been introduced in 1954, the hundred-thousandth Transporter left the assembly line on October 9, 1954 amid a celebration. German was the world soccer champion, and the T1 had now become known

Unlike the standard TAF-T fire engine, the SO 11 flatbed with DL 10 turntable ladder by the Meyer firm of Hagen found little use in firefighting, even though an added "hand-extended ladder" could be mounted, giving a working height of 12 meters. *Photo: Volkswagen Auto Museum Foundation*

almost all over the world. Even in East Germany it had become, thanks to the new "Interzone Trade" regulations of the early autumn of 1951, a rare but all the more popular workhorse from the capitalistic West.

Since the daily production of, at most, 153 T1s could not come close to meeting the demand, a plan was developed in 1954 to build a new Transporter factory outside Wolfsburg. The chosen locality was Hannover-Stoecken, with an infrastructure that was exemplary for its day. Besides direct links with the A2 Autobahn and the Mittelland Canal, the location, very close to the great supplier firms of Varta and Continental, helped to make it the chosen site.

The work at the 120,000 square meter site was tremendous: By the beginning of test production in January 1956, 1,750,000 cubic meters of soil had to be moved, and 120,000 tons of cement

and 28,000 tons of structural steel had to be used, plus 600,000 square meters of wood for casting concrete and more than eight million cinder blocks to form the facades. But before the first T1 could leave the new works, a thorough modification of models was carried out by March 1, 1955. The new modifications already introduced for the Ambulance were now included in the other models. The clearly lower engine space, made possible by a modified air filter, was used for the big rear hatch, and the engine cover was made smaller. More for reasons of space than safety, the fuel tank was moved over the rear axle, so that it no longer had to be filled laboriously via the engine compartment, but could have its own filler cap in the right rear fender. The spare wheel was also located behind the driver's seat to save space. The load capacity thus grew to 4.80 cubic meters.

(opposite page) Production was booming: In 1962 the Hannover works turned out more than 750 Transporters a day for over 130 countries, and more than 5000 engines were built. The work force had grown to 20,000 employees since the production facility was opened six years before. *Photo: Volkswagen Auto Museum Foundation*

Production of the VW Bus began in Wolfsburg on March 8, 1950. Thanks to a self-bearing, all-steel body and cab-over steering, the first VW delivery van became a milestone of light utility vehicles in 1949. With an initial price of comparably favorable 5850 DM (US $1400), it laid the cornerstone for the motorizing of countless artisan and service businesses. *Photo: Volkswagen Auto Museum Foundation*

Further improvements involved the side flap doors, the locks now integrated into the door handles, and the roof, which was fitted with an intake over the windshield to take in fresh air. Inside, the dashboard, now a full-size instrument panel, was dominated by a bigger speedometer. In addition, an electric starter switch replaced the earlier button. For considerably higher riding comfort, the springs on the rear axle were enlarged and equipped with telescopic shock absorbers. Working together with the new 15-inch wheels, they gave results similar to the Beetle's smooth ride. The Bus and Kombi became more important in the realm of large-family driving.

In 1955 the T1 also ventured onto the rails. To increase the mobility of their track-maintenance staffs, the Deutsche Bundesbahn ordered from the Beilhack and WMD a total of thirty railcars based on the T1. While the engine and body were taken directly from the T1, the vehicles were fitted with special railroad chassis "down below," with non-steering axles and railroad wheels. With the help of a lifting apparatus mounted under the vehicle's floor, the railroad service vehicles, called Klv 20-5001 to Klv 20-5030, could be removed from the rails at any place or turned to reverse their direction. The top speed of the 1500 kg "Red Growlers" was 70 kph, with which they could fit into time-table speeds even on main lines. The vehicles held up well, and the last of them were not mustered out until the mid-seventies.

A view of the assembly hall at the new Transporter works in Hannover-Stoecken in 1956. A modest start was made with a work force of 4954 men. Only ten years later, 21,649 workers were on the job here. *Photo: Volkswagen Auto Museum Foundation*

On March 9, 1956 the manager of the new factory in Hannover, Otto Höhne, gave the key for the first Transporter finished there–a flatbed–to VW wholesale dealer Dost of Hildesheim. *Photo: Volkswagen Auto Museum Foundation*

In a great celebration, the 100,000th Transporter came off the assembly line in Wolfsburg on October 9, 1954. It was a good reason for VW General Manager Heinrich Nordhoff to enliven the occasion with a speech to the workers and invited guests. *Photo: Volkswagen Auto Museum Foundation*

In the spring of 1956 there was finally a "big event" in Hannover, as well. On that day, just six years after the beginning of series production, the first T1 officially built in the new factory, a flatbed, rolled off the assembly line. The daily production was at first 250 vehicles, and could be raised step by step to 500 units. Helped by the German Economic Miracle and a simultaneous enlivening in the important export countries of the USA and the Netherlands, even this number was no longer sufficient to cover the increasing worldwide demand for Transporters. On November 1, 1957 the 300,000th T1 had already left the factory. Yearly production in Hannover grew in the same year to 90,000-vehicles, 19,000 of which were exported to the USA. By introducing further market-oriented variations, such as the SO 1 vendor's van or the SO 13 luggage van, the numbers could be increased further. Additional special vehicles were also developed, ranging from the long-goods carrier to the traffic supervision van, leaving scarcely an area of use unfilled.

On November 1, 1958, engine assembly, still taking place in Wolfsburg until then, was also moved to Hannover. Only two years later, Volkswagen introduced its own double cab, based in shape on the model formerly built by Binz. Because of heightened safety regulations in the USA, all vehicles exported there were fitted with special bumpers with ramming protectors, which were also made optionally available for the European market a little later. The introduction of electric directional lights for a higher price, on the other hand, was only a footnote. In October 1958, the pick-up program was extended with a wider metal bed and a wooden bed made by Westfalen in Wiedenbrück, As of 1960, there was also a tipping version with reinforced frame and hydraulic tipping mechanism. Raising the rear bed was done by simple pumping movements on the principle of an auto jack, so that dumped cargoes could now be delivered easily by a one-man crew.

Competition was still vigorous in West Germany. In Europe as well, the economy was improving again. After the European Coal and Steel Community, founded in April 1951, had encouraged this economic advance happen, the Treaty of Rome agreements that took effect on January 1, 1958, became the basic manifesto of the European Economic Community (EEC) for further growth of intra-European trade. With the formation of the EEC came a whole series of national promotional programs linked with the main themes of energy saving and housing construction, and the utilitarian vehicle business also profited from them.

For work on the underside of the vehicle assemblers could adjust the height with a convenient handle control. *Photo: Volkswagen Auto Museum Foundation*

By the end of 1959 the moving of engine production to the Hannover works was finished. On August 1, 1960 production was switched to the new 34 HP engine for Types 1 and 2, after its production for the Transporter had begun on June 1. *Photo: Volkswagen Auto Museum Foundation*

Above: On March 25, 1959 the assembly of the EA 67 engine type had begun in the new production plant. Since May 19 of that year it had been installed in the VW Transporter. The assembly of the old 30 HP engine for Type 1 passenger cars moved to the new location on June 15, 1959, so that, as of December 15, all engine production had moved to Hannover.
*Photo: Volkswagen Auto Museum Foundation*

Left: Production goes on in the summer of 1959: In Hall 2 was the circle-shaped engine test bench. Its measuring equipment met the highest demands in precision.
*Photo: Volkswagen Auto Museum Foundation*

Right: The curved bumpers for the heightened safety regulations in the USA were soon available at extra cost for European vehicles as well.
*Photo: Volkswagen Auto Museum Foundation*

In the mid-fifties, the Hannover works already stood out as a modern automobile factory. When the parts were not moved by belts or cranes, transport was done for the most part on the floor under the production rooms. This concept provided much room between the moving bands. *Photo: Volkswagen Auto Museum Foundation*

One of the best-known photo series is the series of motifs called "Camping Bus in Gifhorn." *Photo: Volkswagen Auto Museum Foundation*

On August 21, 1959, the 50,000th VW employee was hired at the Hannover works, and just four days later the 500,000th T1 was produced. On June 29, 1960, the German Bundestag at long last voted by a large majority to turn the state-owned Volkswagen GmbH into a privately financed Volkswagen AG. Only a few weeks later, on August 22, 1960, came the registering of the new business in the trade register at the Wolfsburg court house. Forty per cent of the shares, each with a nominal value of 100 DM, were shared by the nation and the state of Niedersachsen. The remaining 60% were "scattered far" according to the parliamentary decision, but a great many of them ended up in the hands of influential members of the Porsche family.

With the standard introduction of electric directional lights and the resulting end of the old-type blinkers, the breakthrough into modern times began for the T1 that year. The introduction of asymmetrical low beams provided better vision on the road. The pressure of the windshield washers was increased and the power of the wiper motor was raised. A starting repeat block was introduced that protected against damage to the starter. The high-compression engine now produced 34 HP and was fitted with optimal cold-start running with a comfortable automatic starter instead of earlier choke. A cherry-picker made by the Ruthmann firm in Gescher and intended for municipal and maintenance work was introduced in June 1960 and completed the list of special bodies. The cherry-picker truck, based on the flatbed, had an electric, hydraulically operated basket with a maximum carrying power of 150 kg and a working height of 7.50 meters. With a base price of almost 16,000 DM (US $4000), the Ruthmann cherry-picker has for many years been the most expensive Volkswagen delivered from the works.

In 1951, two years after the first VW bus appeared, VW introduced the luxurious "Small Bus Special Version" with windows in the roof panels and a folding hatch cover. The "Samba" was designed solely to carry people and quickly became a popular vehicle among smaller bus companies for city tours and short trips into nearby countries. *Photo: Volkswagen Auto Museum Foundation*

An advertising photo from the fifties: The newly attained mobility lured many Germans to vacation spots in the south in those times. But this picture was taken in a studio before a photo background. *Photo: Volkswagen Auto Museum Foundation*

On the road with an assembly troop on working days, on a picnic with the family on weekends—with an additional row of seats in the cargo space, the Transporter became a real "Multi-Van." *Photo: Volkswagen Auto Museum Foundation*

In 1961, directional, brake, and backup lights were combined in an oval housing for all models. In addition, the tie rods of the front axle no longer needed servicing. Features on the interior included a sunshade on the passenger's side and a fuel gauge on the instrument panel. With that the fuel shutoff valve that dated back to the early days of automobiling was eliminated. To make the T1 usable for larger freight items, a larger box van with a roof height of 2285 mm was added to the array of models as of September 1961. One year later, the Clinomobil firm of Hannover rebuilt the larger box van into the first forerunner of the present-day ambulance or rescue vehicle. To be sure, mobile rescue squads were still in their infancy at that time, so that neither surgery nor acutely needed life-sustaining measures could be done while the vehicle was in motion.

Along with municipal and rescue use, recreational activities were also taking on more and more importance for Volkswagen. After the "Camping Wagon SO 23," built by Westfalia since 1959, found numerous buyers in Germany and elsewhere, the Wiedenbrück firm expanded its range of fully different, and differently priced, camping vehicles based on the T1 at the beginning of 1961, with their "SO 22 Mosaic" build-it-yourself furnishings. The array extended from a simple "Bus with Bed" to a luxurious SO 44: with refrigerator, running water, and Dormobil roof tent structure (as of 1965). Since only few people in the Old World could afford such luxury, the man market for these special vehicles was in the USA, which is why two different interior furnishings were offered for many models. While the European customers preferred an interior with real wood finish, the Americans chose bright and washable plastic surfaces.

A production record in the building of utility vehicles. Only 12 years after its introduction, the millionth VW Transporter was finished on October 2, 1962. Production manager Otto Höhne praised this accomplishment before the factory staff and the press. The jubilee model–a Samba Bus–was a gift of the VW works to UNICEF. *Photo: Volkswagen Auto Museum Foundation*

With the building of the Berlin wall in August 1961, the Germans in the east no longer had the freedom to travel. Millions of dissatisfied DDR residents, including many younger and better-qualified workers left their country after the 1953 workers' uprising and headed for West Germany. To prevent a further "sell-out" of their own state, the Ulbricht government sealed their borders almost hermetically. Commercial activities with the West were also frozen for the most part, whereby the purchase of Volkswagen vehicles in the self-proclaimed "workers' and farmers' state" came to an abrupt end.

In 1962 the Volkswagen AG added a third series, the Type 3, to its delivery program. The "big VW," as the 1500 was called, was available as a sedan, variant, and coupe, and had a newly developed boxer engine with a fan wheel attached directly to the crankshaft. Parallel to the appearance of the VW 1500, the 42 HP aggregate was also offered in the T1, although, for space reasons, it had the usual fan, as before. The 34 HP engine of the Beetle remained available, the firm wanted to wait for customer reactions at first. Because of the higher torque of 95 Nm at 2000 rpm, a larger clutch disc of 200 mm diameter completed the factory "tuning." In the cab, an adjustable single seat and a folding double seat replaced the earlier "sofa." The designers were also able to enlarge the front foot space slightly by altering the headlight cutouts as part of the model's modification. A decisive new feature was the introduction of a separated air intake system for engine cooling and interior heating, so that the heated air no longer was used first to cool the engine, but was taken in separately. Thus the lingering oil smell during heating was finally gone. The new model year was externally recognizable by the bigger wheel wells and a bead over the rear wheel boxes. In the same year, a Samba bus was the millionth Transporter to leave the factory, going into service for UNICEF.

1963 brought the end of the Adenauer era and the introduction of the thoroughly revised T1c. For the first time in T1 typology, a newly designed sliding side door could be chosen for a higher price, instead of the normal side door. Only at a second look does one notice the ventilation louvers that incline inward and the bigger directional lights at the front, which, despite their harmonious total effect, were satirized as "frog-eyes" or "fried eggs." In back, a wider rear hatch with a push-button latch and an enlarged window offered much more loading comfort and a better rear view. The reinforced front axle, available only in the Transporter 1500 until then, was now standard for all models. Tubeless 7.00-14 tires of 5J x 14 size were to guarantee better roadholding. For more even braking, each axle was given four equally large drum brakes. With the introduction of a new one-ton version, offered only along with the more powerful 42 HP engine, Volkswagen expanded its offerings of utility vehicles into the next higher weight class.

Many Volkswagens also served Lufthansa as follow-me vehicles, shuttles, or luggage transporters in past decades. Here a T1 stands just in front of a Vickers V-814 Viscount, which was used for long hauls by Lufthansa from 1958 to 1971. The lettering on the Transporter was not attached by adhesive foil then as now, but hand-painted. *Photo: German Lufthansa AG*

Only one model year later, the T1 was updated again. Besides increased comfort, the main feature added by the engineers was increased safety. A hand-operated windshield washer was now standard, as were bigger and stronger wiper blades that switched off into final position. After experiencing engine damage from over-revving, both vehicles were fitted with governors. Larger heat exchangers were also installed for better heating. At the year's end, an easily handled plastic roof finally replaced the old velour cover. All this fine work was appreciated by the customers, as the sales figures show. In 1964 the T1 sales reach a new high point of 200,325 vehicles. This impelled Ford of Cologne to give up the costly new development of an FK 1000 successor and instead to take over the short-hood Transit designed by Ford of England.

In 1965, Volkswagen introduced the Type 147, a little brother to the T1 designed specially for the German Bundespost. Since the development of the T2 was already going strong, there was much speculation among the public as to whether the "Fridolin" mail truck could represent a small copy of the new T2. So as not to let sales decline in view of these reports, the T1 was carefully upgraded again. As of August 1965, the 1500 cc engine was given larger valves and now produced 44 HP. In addition, a stronger generator with inserted contacts provided for a more steadily working electric system. Also in the electric realm were the two windshield wiper motors, the new combination lever for directionals, high beams, and flashers. The typical VW foot dimmer switch was gone. The front side doors gained separate inside opening handles, and the mirror was modified to match the larger rear window added in 1963. Much more permanent, though, were the changes to the suspension, where a new front stabilizer and identical telescopic shock absorbers helped to diminish the annoying "turning in" under full braking. Since the Beetle engine no longer played a noteworthy role in orders, it was removed from the price list for good in October 1965.

The T1 entered its last year in August 1966 with a new 12-volt generator and numerous detail changes in the interior. Thanks to the newly introduced one-key system, clumsy fumbling with various types of keys was finally eliminated. For the export market, a two-circuit brake system was available for the first time. The mechanics were also overhauled one last time. In January 1967 a crankshaft with double oil channels in a cross-form and a new main crankshaft bearing with a second oil channel were introduced. At the beginning of

the 1967 factory vacation, production of the T1
ended in Germany, after 1,800,000 vehicles had
been built. In Brazil, though, production remained
unchanged until 1975. The successor of the T1
appeared as the eagerly awaited T2.

This Type 23 Kombi built in 1953, a so-called "flat-nose," already has the opening window with crank introduced that year. The vehicle was finally restored after more than 30 years and is still used occasionally for everyday driving. *Photo: Jörg Hajt*

The rear end of the Kombi is, unfortunately, not completely original, as an accident in the 1960s ruined the simple lights. For many younger Bulli fans, this is an unusual sight: the engine hood that was lacking until 1955.

This T1b, built in 1961, was a former ray-detecting vehicle of the German Red Cross, with the original 33,000 km on the odometer. When it was restored, the vehicle was converted to a very elegant minibus. *Photo: Jörg Hajt*

Practical: The big side doors allow easy access to the passenger area. *Photo: Jörg Hajt*

"It is a pleasure car and a business vehicle, a family car and a camping wagon," said VW advertising for the finely kept T1c passenger transporter. The elegant color combination of sea blue and lotus white of the vehicle shown here, though, was available only since 1965. *Photo: Jörg Hajt*

With its rear hatch enlarged by almost a third, the T1c could not only be loaded better, but also looked much more modern. The hatch was opened by a simple push-button. The turning handle and the half-moon handle recess are gone. *Photo: Jörg Hajt*

The first Type 22 and 28 passenger transporters already had two-tone paint and were fitted with a "solid, tasteful, and sound-damping all-over covering." Surely nobody thought in 1955 that the seats would later be covered in genuine leather. *Photo: Walter Heinrich*

Thanks to elegant two-tone paint and chrome trim, the "Samba Bus" made a very tasteful impression from the rear too. Today this model, with a market value of some 50,000 Euros (US $65,500), ranks among the most desirable of all VW Transporters. *Photo: Jörg Hajt*

With the "Small Bus Special Version," better known in popular parlance as the "Samba Bus," VW introduced a luxurious eight-seater with panoramic windows and sun roof in 1951. This vehicle was built in 1952 and is one of the most perfect examples of the German T1 passion. *Photo: Jörg Hajt*

Above: This T1b Type 22 passenger transporter ranked among the most widespread T1 types then as now. This one was built in 1962 and is in its original form since being restored. *Photo: Jörg Hajt*

Left: The oval rear lights show that this passenger transporter was built after 1961. At the same time, the half-moon-shaped handle recess above the rear hatch handle was introduced. *Photo: Jörg Hajt*

With a full-length rear bed of 4.20 square meters, the pick-up proved to be very useful for large transport tasks. No wonder that the truck shown here was still used occasionally for everyday tasks until a few years ago.
*Photo: Jörg Hajt*

This Type 26 pick-up built in 1963 was owned by an Italian olive farmer. The truck was hand-restored in 2000 and still has its original engine with 34 HP and has covered fewer than 95,000 kilometers.
*Photo: Jörg Hajt*

With an original 348 km on the odometer, this double-cab Type 265 of 1960 was "forgotten" at a VW dealership and is one of the rarest VW Transporters worldwide. Of course the truck is still technically and optically as good as new. *Photo: Jörg Hajt*

The rear view of this "Pritschenbus," particularly popular among artisans and gardeners, looks almost filigreed from the back. Some years ago, there was a similar version on the market, made by Binz in Lorch. *Photo: Jörg Hajt*

With a contemporary Böcker roofer's conveyor-belt trailer, this T1c double-cab Type 2616 pickup of 1964 looks like new. A roll-up top provides weather protection for the load, so that even water-sensitive materials can be carried. The separation of the side windows, unlike those of the T1b double-cab, is easy to see. *Photo: Jörg Hajt*

In place of the obligatory "treasure chest" of the normal pick-up, the double-cab has a gas filler. The vehicle shown here uses the 1.6-liter engine with 50 HP. *Photo: Jörg Hajt*

In the time of the Economic Miracle, advertising signs already typified the appearance of many utilitarian vehicles, like this T1b bottle truck, which advertises Florida Boy soft drinks, no longer available today. *Photo: Jörg Hajt*

Simple but useful: On the chassis of the normal Type 26 pick-up, various body-building firms produced special stacking terraces to hold numerous boxes. Depending on the customer's wants and pocketbook, the rear body could be made of wood or metal. *Photo: Jörg Hajt*

After being left alone for decades, this Type 26 "Covered Pick-Up" in original condition could be bought in the 1990s by its present owner for only 400 Marks (US $235). After appropriate touching up, the rare vehicle gleams again as when it was delivered in 1953. *Photo: Stefan Gross*

From behind as well, the sturdy pick-up looks as if it just came from the showroom. The simple taillights and central brake light touch the heart of any Bulli fan. Despite its great age, the vehicle is still used occasionally on the premises of a flower nursery. *Photo: Stefan Gross*

Right: As usual in vehicles with prewar technology, the first generation of VW Transporters had a starting crank. *Photo: Stefan Gross*

Since the box van as a purely utilitarian vehicle was exposed to much wear, few have reached their retirement years. The photo shows a second-generation Type 21 "Delivery Van" originally used in Lausanne. It is painted a "loud" color rarely seen on a T1b. *Photo: Tom Aebersold*

For the promotional tours proclaimed as "Housewife Advising" to advertise their baking products, the grocery firm of Dr. Oetker kept a goodly number of VW Transporters. This T1b box van keeps the memories alive, and is seen here with a contemporary Westfalia two-wheel trailer. *Photo: Walter Heinrich*

This T1c of the Düsseldorf Rheinbahn AG service truck, ideally restored in 1998, is treasured by the historical "Linie De.V." work group. It was originally an equipment carrier of the Bremervörde volunteer fire company and was put into service in 1967. *Photo: Jörg Hajt*

Almost as in olden times: The Rheinbahn T1 is at work, meeting an equally historical 1289 streetcar. *Photo: Jörg Hajt*

Above: The red US taillights of this box van, thoroughly restored in 2003, like the striking two-tone paint, pay homage to the legendary VW buses of the American Flower Power generation. *Photo: Jörg Hajt*

Left: The basis for this T1c in the style of the US cult tuner EMPI was a 44 HP TSF 1 fire truck with a gross weight of a stately 2150 kg, put into service in 1966. *Photo: Jörg Hajt*

Above: Again as a delivery van without relocated directionals, this T1b box van of 1956 bears the logo of a contemporary farm produce firm. *Photo: Archives*

Left: The Type 22 and 28 minibuses differ from the Kombiwagen at first glance by their standard two-tone paint. Inside, full coverings with sound damping provide appropriate comfort. *Photo: Walter Heinrich*

Opposite, above: This VW Type SO 33, built by the Westfalia firm in Wiedenbrück in 1962, is an "old school" type. The bus has kept its original 34-PS engine to this day. *Photo: Jörg Hajt*

Opposite, below: Typical of the practical interior of the SO 33 was, besides the well-planned space division, the successful blend of various-colored oak furnishings. *Photo: Jörg Hajt*

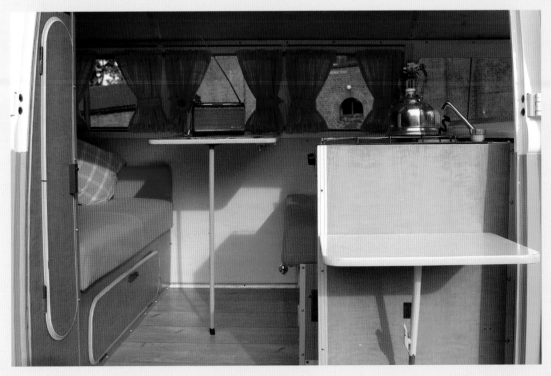

Camping, as in the sixties, is allowed by this Westfalia SO 34 "Flip Seat" Camping Wagon in restored condition with all its equipment. The vehicle was taken to the USA in 1964 by a German CIA employee through a shadowy importer, reaching its present owner by way of Britain. *Photo: Jörg Hajt*

Fine work: the bar of the Westfalia SO 34 with typical glasses of its time. *Photo: Jörg Hajt*

Quiet corner: Original Westfalia camping toilet in the combined WC and changing tent. *Photo: Jörg Hajt*

Spartan: The dashboard with Blaupunkt "Frankfurt" radio and "Made in USA" bottle holder. *Photo: Jörg Hajt*

Typical of the sixties: Colorful couches of the SO 34 equipment package. *Photo: Jörg Hajt*

Pure travel is exemplified by this splendidly restored "Type 23 Kombi as Camping Wagon" with a large tent and the spare-time utensils needed for a perfect vacation. Note the use of a big roof rack along with the roof hatch. *Photo: Tom Sebersold*

Unrestored and with its original paint, this Westfalia Camping Wagon of 1966 is seen in the SO 44 luxury version with Dormobil raising roof and six sleeping places. The front bumper bars indicate the US version. *Photo: Jörg Hajt*

A big rear hatch and little inside it. Since the engine hood of the SO 44 was also planned as a place to sleep, there is little storage space available for the travelers. *Photo: Jörg Hajt*

Another SO 44 with Dormobil body is this superbly maintained Camping Bus of 1965. To increase the storage space, the spare wheel was simply mounted on the nose, which often resulted in denting of the front bodywork. *Photo: Jörg Hajt*

The fiberglass-reinforced plastic hinged roof made by Dormobil, held by three metal clamps, includes three opening ventilation windows with sewn-in mosquito nets. *Photo: Jörg Hajt*

This Type 23, finished in March 1967, incorporates the last body type of the Westfalia Camping Bus on T1 chassis. Obligatory in this model was the shortened Westfalia roof rack, here loaded with contemporary vacation equipment. The bus stayed with its first owner from 1967 to 1989 and was restored lavishly by its present owner in 1993-94. *Photo: Jörg Hajt*

A look at the kitchen with its gas stove and sink. *Photo: Jörg Hajt*

A breezy hotel on wheels: for reaching its full height, a small raising roof in the middle of the vehicle replaced the earlier hinged roof as of 1965. Also included in the SO 44 equipment was the sleeping place seen here atop the engine hood. *Photo: Jörg Hajt*

No longer an everyday scene, this Type 261 flatbed was made in 1967 with its five-year-older long-load rack and SO 24 trailer from the Ficker vehicle factory in Neuenhaus. For smaller artisan businesses in particular, this rig offered a good alternative to a bigger truck. *Photo: Jörg Hajt*

With its pivoting rack, the transport carriage can be effortlessly maneuvered through narrow streets and entranceways. *Photo: Jörg Hajt.*

Unlike the SO 24, the SO 14 long-load transport trailer is made simply as a trailer with rungs. The turning mechanism, though, is the same, as seen on a double-cab truck built for the Portuguese market in 1966 and later equipped with Porsche wheels. *Photo: Stefan Gross*

The swiveling-ladder DL 10, built by Meyer of Hagen and in the VW program since 1953, was especially popular among roofers and electricians. With a working height of 10 meters, the manual climbing help was suitable even for impressive roadway construction. *Photo: Walter Heinrich*

Left: In fully functional, unrestored original condition, this Type 261 pickup, built in 1965 and carrying a Ruthmann Type V 60 cherry-picker, has reliably put in its service for Energy Production of Eastern Bavaria for more than three decades. *Photo: Jörg Hajt*

Below: With a sales price of barely 19,500 DM (US $4875), the Ruthmann cherry-picker was the most expensive model in the T1 range. Thus the vehicle, produced in Gescher, Westphalia, was used mainly by municipalities and energy supply companies. *Photo: Jörg Hajt*

In August 1963, VW introduced the third generation of the standard "21F TSF" fire engine, which, with its allowable gross weight of 2150 kg, could carry the heaviest load of any fire engine up to that time. Thanks to its comparatively favorable selling price, it replaced the prewar fire trucks for many factory firefighters. *Photo: Walter Heinrich*

The world's most terrible T1 is surely this "Mental Breakdown" dragster, even though it has only the cab of a Bulli. With 1700 HP from 8400 cc of displacement, it can reach speeds like those of a jet plane. *Photo: HFD*

Along with town and welfare services, numerous factory fire companies in Germany and beyond bought the VW Ambulance. This photo shows a Type 27 put into service in 1962 by the Sandoz firm in Switzerland, with its original blue dome light. *Photo: Walter Heinrich*

The first box van from the Hannover works was this 21F Kombi crew car made in 1956. The photo shows it after its restoration as a fire truck of the Eveshausen volunteer fire company. *Photo: Jörg Hajt*

Rear view of the 21F with original simple taillights and Westfalia roof rack to carry fire hose. *Photo: Jörg Hajt*

The folding seat near the door served in emergencies for quick opening of the folding doors. The sliding door, actually meant for quick exit, was available only since 1963. *Photo: Jörg Hajt*

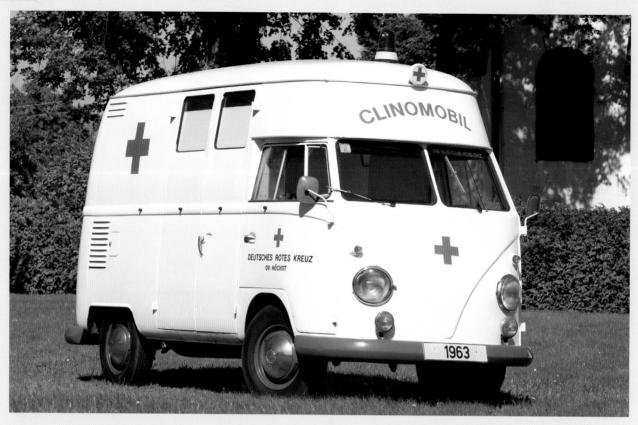

Based on the M 222 large-space box van, the Clinomobil Works in Hannover developed the "Clinomobil," the forerunner of the present-day rescue ambulance, in 1962. Mobile rescue squads, of course, were very new in those days, and neither operations nor life-sustaining treatments could be carried out while in motion. *Photo: Jörg Hajt*

Because of the high roof and the rear hatch that had to be opened wide in the original M 222 model, the Clinomobil could do without cost-intensive body modifications. *Photo: Jörg Hajt*

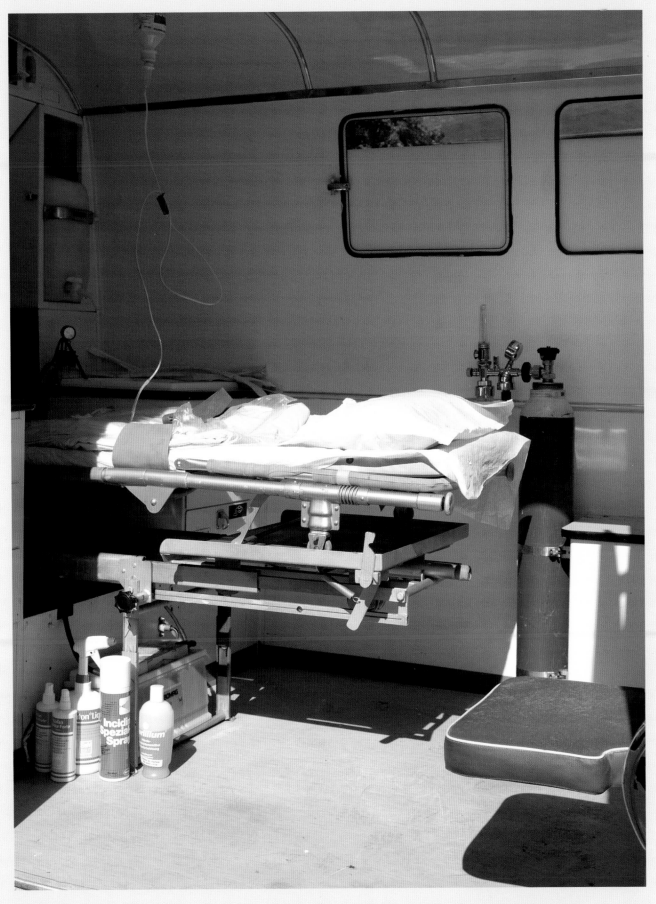

A look at the medical treatment equipment in the unrestored original state of the Clinomobil, which seems extremely Spartan and limited in comparison with present-day rescue vehicles. *Photo: Jörg Hajt*

The filigreed holding bow of the ladder also plays a stabilizing role for the body. Also well-planned is the convenient access to the water pump, which was made in Germany. *Photo: Jörg Hajt*

Typical of the countless VW Transporters with foreign bodies this T1a fire truck is by the Belgian coachbuilder Andre Ilians of Alken. It is in unrestored original condition. *Photo: Jörg Hajt*

The body of this fire engine used by the Belgian Cristal Brewery from 1955 to 1995 was made of a normal box van while retaining the basic body shape. *Photo: Jörg Hajt*

Typical of railroads, these railcars have a red light on the back. The brake light over the license plate was retained all the same. *Photo: Mathias Bootz, Railroad Equipment, Bad Nauheim*

Since the Klv 20 was conceived as a one-direction vehicle, it could change its direction with the help of an extendable hydraulic stamp with a turning plate. *Photo: Markus Schmidt, Bootz Collection*

For the German Bundesbahn, the firms of Beilhack and WMD built a total of 30 railcars of the Klv 20 series in 1955, based on the T1. This photo shows the superbly restored Klv 20 of the Butzbach-Licher Railroad Friends. *Photo: Mathias Bootz, Railroad Supplies, Bad Nauheim*

# The VW T2 Bus (1967-1979)

## THE NEXT GENERATION APPEARS …

# The VW T2 Bus (1967-1979)
## THE NEXT GENERATION APPEARS …

A double-cab version was also foreseen for the array of models in the second Transporter generation. The early prototype shown here dates back to 1967. *Photo: Volkswagen Auto Museum Foundation*

The development of the second Transporter generation took almost three years and was characterized by an economically difficult situation. The quickly worsening recession, with a high financial deficit and quickly rising workers' salaries, led to great insecurity in the economy as well as among the population. For the responsible parties at VW, these were not good prerequisites for having a new vehicle developed, and the actual developmental work also did not run as planned. Besides constantly recurring hairline cracks in the self-bearing body and massive difficulties with its rigidity, such important points as crash safety and the effectiveness of the newly developed safety steering could not be solved satisfactorily at first. But also presumably simple components, such as the rain gutter over the windshield, gave the

designers more headaches than were expected. Torrents of water poured over the windshield again and again when braking in the rain, which required numerous changes in the gutter shape. But by the official start of production of the new T2 on August 1, 1967, this problem, too, had been overcome. The most noticeable difference from the previous model was the clearly smoother front of the vehicle, with a one-piece panoramic windshield and standing headlights. [p. 79] Besides that, the T2, thanks to its body being 140 mm longer with its width unchanged, looked sleeker, which was not only good visually but also provided more storage space. The shape was inspired mainly by the Type 3, while the T1 still showed its development from the Beetle.

The atmosphere of the interior also proved to be long separated from the Beetle. Everything looked much more lavish and modern. Besides a completely new dashboard design with three round instruments and ergonomically arranged controls, the interior, particularly in the bus version, looked more like a sedan. There was also a whole series of new safety features, running from recessed door handles through a windshield washer operated by compressed air to a hand-brake button in the middle of the dashboard in place of the earlier floor-mounted lever.

Bigger side mirrors helped the driver maneuver, and the standard sliding side door provided more comfort for loading and unloading. In the upper part of the C pillars, the cooling air for the engine was now ducted by special wind-direction vanes, eliminating the characteristic louvers of the T1. The larger body and better equipping naturally had a negative effect on the vehicle's weight, which could be compensated for by the reworked boxer engine, now with 47 HP from 1584 cc displacement. The higher weight of 105 kg was balanced by the maximum torque of 106 Nm at 2800 rpm.

With a fully newly designed transverse-link rear axle without reduction gears, the T2 appeared in 1967 as the successor to the successful T1. Riding comfort and driving characteristics were much improved, thanks to the new rear-axle geometry. *Photo: Volkswagen Auto Museum Foundation*

The success story went on: Only five and a half years after the millionth Transporter came off the assembly line, there was another cause for celebration at the Hannover works on February 5, 1968, the finishing of the two millionth vehicle of that type. *Photo: Volkswagen Auto Museum Foundation*

The new rear axle, guided by longitudinal and transverse links with double-joint driveshafts, set new standards for riding comfort similar to a car and provided almost sporting driving characteristics. But the brake system also proved to be excellent for its time: Volkswagen had met the increased safety regulations in large parts of Europe with a standard two-circuit brake system, which is still used in this form in Type 3.

The array of models again included all the body types and special bodies known from the T1. The only exception was the Samba Bus, which was dropped without a replacement. Its former position was taken by the new "Clipper" top model. This luxury bus, available with seven or eight seats, had to get by without a roof window or cloth top. Whoever wanted to let more "light, air and sun" had to go back to the steel sliding roof available on all buses since January 1968. By lacking these exclusive features, the success of the Clipper, priced from 9700 DM (US $2437) up, was well below expectation. After a lost court case against the American Pan Am airline, which had secured the right to the name of the high-sea concept, the luxury T2 was known only as the "Seven-seat L" or "Eight-seat L" in sales brochures–externally recognizable by its chrome trim and standard two-tone paint.

As of August 1972, care of the T2b included special means of improving safety, in that the front disc brakes were now standard equipment, and wider drum brakes on the rear wheels provided improved slowing. Seat belts for all passengers were also standard. *Photo: Volkswagen Auto Museum Foundation*

The double-cab version was an ideal vehicle for municipal motor pools or construction firms. It was produced at the Volkswagen Works itself for the first time in 1958, and not by the Binz firm in Lorch, Wuerttemberg. In the second version it was also a great sales success. *Photo: Volkswagen Auto Museum Foundation*

Despite the base prices, which had risen well above those of the T1 – 6475 Marks for the covered truck, 6890 DM (US $1750) for the Kombi and 7980 DM ($2000) for the Bus – the T2 merged smoothly into the success of its predecessor. It was not only possible to sell the two millionth VW Transporter in 1968, but also the 200,000th T2! This superb start at the head of the European small transporters, despite economic troubles, amazed not only the VW leadership, which was accustomed to success, but also the editors of many well-known auto magazines, who might have wished for more visual distance from the old bus. But as it had with the T1, Volkswagen did not simply stop with this momentary success, but constantly perfected the T2. In 1968 it was given drum brakes with labyrinth sealing between the brake drum and plate for improved wet braking. The performance of the generator was also improved, and a modified gearbox with changed pinion and new equalizing-drive bearings was also used. For better defroster performance, there were newly made air outlet openings under the windshield. The new VW shift pattern, not used in all vehicles, was printed on the ashtray from then on. In the same year the Volkswagen 411 (Type 4) appeared, perhaps the most questionable interpretation of the Wolfsburg rear-engine concept. The heart of the middle-class model, available as a fastback sedan or variant wagon, was a newly developed flat boxer engine with 1700 or 1800 cc displacement and producing 68 to 85 HP.

This is how the basic models of the second-generation VW Transporter looked as of August 1972: Pickups with and without double cab, Kombi and Box Van. *Photo: Volkswagen Auto Museum Foundation*

The 1970 model year began sportily for Volkswagen. With the introduction of the new VW Porsche 914 (Type 47) to the market in the autumn of 1969, the world's first mass-produced medium sports car with the overworked transverse-link rear axle of the T2 appeared against such renowned competitors as the Alfa Romeo Giulia Sprint and Opel GT. At the same time, some of the T2 engine production was moved from Hannover to the newly built Salzgitter works. Surprisingly for many, the T2 soon became the carrier of innovations that extended over production series. In close cooperation with Thyssen Steel, five test cars appeared with a completely galvanized bodies. German know-how for alloying and welding was brought into model production by the Duisburg steel firm. Until well into the eighties, three of these models were produced in factories at Volkswagen and two at Thyssen. In firmly established cycles, the thickness of the zinc coating layers was measured, and the results were later introduced into the production of fully zinc-plated Audi and Porsche bodies.

Through another upgrading of US safety standards, the subject of passive safety also had to be brought back to life. To make the chassis more rigid, the front doors were given an additional brace as of August 1969. The front frames were also made in a Y shape for controlled energy pickup. New means of safe steering were also explored. After the development team around Paul Orbach wanted to introduce an impact-bolt system with Bowden cable for snapping of the steering column when the T2 series began, new tests showed that this effect could be achieved with the help of a simple breaking point.

Further improvements concerned the front directional lights with new rippling, the speedometer with a 100-meter counter, and a make-up mirror in the passenger's sunshade of the bus. In the front doors of all T2 models there were now door contact switches [p. 84] for inside lighting. The opening angles of the door stops were made smaller and the inner lock buttons were moved from the edge of the windows to near the door openers. The gearbox mounts were now made softer, so the vibrations affecting the chassis could be absorbed. To lower the oil temperature, a bigger cross-section of the oil channels and an oil pump with higher performance were planned. Increased braking power was also available for a higher price.

Through the hippie scene that grew out of the new type of student movement and the anti-Vietnam War faction, the Transporter also became political overnight. As "the" means of travel for the active postwar generation, the sometimes colorfully painted T1 and T2 appeared on the "hippie trails" en route to Afghanistan, India, or the US west coast. Even more than the Beetle or Duck, the Bulli thus became a symbol of young people striving for social independence. The responsible persons at Volkswagen were understandably not happy about that. Along with an enormous loss of image, they feared most of all the loss of their conservative customers to "politically correct" competitors' cars and the banning of the Transporter from government service and its large sales. To be sure, such fears were fully unfounded, as the growing sales figures showed.

The space concept of the T2 Kombi was laid out for a total of up to nine people. The "VW Person Transporter" with seven seats sold for 8490 DM (US $2360) in the first production year, the eight-seat version for 8540 DM, and the nine-seater was listed at 8590 DM. *Photo: Volkswagen Auto Museum Foundation*.

German politics also brought far-reaching changes. With the election of Willy Brandt as the first German Chancellor with a social-liberal coalition, the foundation was laid for a new reform policy. "Dare more democracy" was the motto in those days. East Germany was recognized as a second German nation by the Brandt administration. Acknowledgment of the Western nations and the wish for an understanding with the other Warsaw Pact members helped to assure peace. While the first half of the 1960s was typified by saber-rattling and fear of a world war, the policy of relaxing was now in the foreground of political action. The Federal Republic was more colorful, which surely was not due only to the Prilflowers introduced in 1972! The happy spirit of the times also made cars more colorful: orange, yellow and green were the new fashion colors.

In 1970, the production of the K70 was begun in the Salzgitter works. In the same year the T2 became stronger. By deliberate work on the cylinder heads and a new recirculated-air carburetor, the engine power rose to 50 HP. The oil overheating that still occurred was dealt with by reworking the oil pump again for greater flow through it, plus a newly designed, thermostat-controlled oil-bath air filter. In the former version, the shape of the oil cooler hindered the supplying of cool air, so that it often overheated. The results were severe engine damage such as a "piston-eater" [p. 85] or the tearing off of the outlet valve plate. For fine filtering of dirt particles from the motor oil, a newly developed cleaning cartridge with a paper filter set into it was used.

In August 1963, VW advertising declared that the T1 was both "a pleasure car and a business vehicle, a family car and a camping wagon." The same applied to the T2 series, since it clearly offered more riding comfort and also noticeably more comfort from its furnishings. *Photo: Volkswagen Auto Museum Foundation*

The T2 was freshened up visually by new 5.5 J x 14 wheels with a smaller circle of holes and flatter Type 3 hubcaps. Although the tire width remained the same, the wheel wells and spare holder were made for the new wheel size. The three-armed pressure plate without a press-on ring, built into the declutching bearing of the clutch, also came from the Type 3. The now-standard disc brakes on the front axle added greater safety. Beyond that, the larger brake drums on the rear axles, made of steel instead of cast iron, were made for a longer life cycle. To keep the braking effect the same, even when carrying a load, the rear axle was given a brake-power regulator. Thus the allowable load limit could also be raised. The year of 1970 ended for the T2 with two new records. In all, 80,354 Transporters found buyers in Germany, while 72,515 were exported to the USA. This event would never be equaled in the rear-engine era! Despite that, many details of the

T2 were reworked in 1971. The result of this first large-scale upgrading was the symbiosis, known today as the "Zwitterbus," of the T2a and T2b. For greater ground clearance with the same overall height, the roof was flattened slightly. The front fenders were slightly widened, which made the Transporter look more "bullish." The oval taillights gave way to [p. 86] a narrow vertical band of lights. The rear air intakes were enlarged and now had nine louvers instead of seven. The engine cover was redesigned and given a new emblem area. For safety reasons, the fuel filler was moved farther back, out of the danger area of the sliding door. The Bus and L versions were immediately fitted with regulated ventilators in the front doors. In the bus, the turning window in the passenger area was eliminated. Much attention was also given to improved sound damping. The power unit was mounted on rubber, and the tank and engine areas were lined with damping material.

Optionally, the Bulli could be bought as a dumper with the normal tipper or the large wooden rear body, which had a 5.2 square meter bed, offering almost a square meter more of space. The dumper could be ordered with hydraulic-mechanical or hydraulic-electric dumping activation. *Photo: Volkswagen Auto Museum Foundation*

Beyond that, the age of computers began in Hannover. The T2 was one of the first German automobiles to be fitted with a diagnostic plug-in. The most important optional innovation was the Type 4 1700 cc flat engine with a dual carburetor system. It larger size required the filling tube to bemoved forward 25 mm and the rear axle element was fitted correspondingly. Since this was not possible in the flatbed trucks, the flat engine was not offered for these. The [p. 88] engine power was 66 HP at 4800 rpm; the maximum torque was 113 Nm at 3200 rpm. The extra power, of course, was gained from higher fuel consumption. Consumption values of 15 liters per 100 km were seen as normal and were some 20% higher than those of the standard transmission. To handle the new top performance, a braking-power enhancer and 185 SR 14 belted tires were added. For braking with the increased power, the main brake and rear wheel brake cylinders were larger. External marks of the Type 4 aggregate were its big exhaust pipe on the passenger's side plus (as of August 1972) the removable adjustment lid for the two downdraft Solex carburetors in the cargo space. Because of the modified mounting of the engine and gearbox, the rear and bottom components

From 1972 on, automatic shifting was available for the Bulli. The three-speed automatic transmission could be had along with the flat 62 HP engine, which was developed from that of the VW 411/412. *Photo: Volkswagen Auto Museum Foundation*

were reinforced, independently of the engine, with stiffer panels, supports, and additional carriers – recognizable from outside by the more angular rear bodywork. In addition, a [p. 89] low-wear membrane clutch plate replaced the three-arm clutch without a pressure ring that had been added just a year before.

The closed box van with its loading floor of 4.1 square meters could carry a volume of five cubic meters. The high-roof box van with the same floor added another 1.2 cubic meters of space. *Photo: Volkswagen Auto Museum Foundation*

As with the covered T1, the sidewalls of the T2 variant could also be lowered all the way without troublesome hinges sticking out. *Photo: Volkswagen Auto Museum Foundation*

In September 1971 the three millionth VW Transporter was built. It was, thus, the most successful utility vehicle in automotive history. Yet the enthusiasm was kept within limits. The danger of bankruptcy hovered over the Volkswagen firm. The formerly profitable business was in the worst crisis of its existence. Sales of the Beetle hit a new depth, and the two other large-volume vehicles, the 1500/1600 and 411, and the K70 recently acquired from NSU, passed it in the market. In 1971 Volkswagen lost the lead in the German market to Opel, which matched the spirit of the times just right with their Kadett, Ascona, and Manta models. Volkswagen did not have much to set against them. A loud rear engine, limited space, and a simple design no longer lured car buyers to

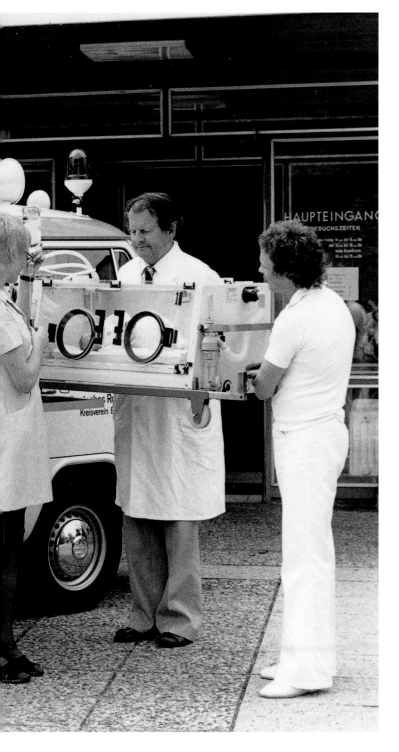

The special versions of the T2 were very popular among the police, firefighters, and rescue services. Special versions like this emergency baby doctor's vehicle were usually built by the Binz body specialists. *Photo: Volkswagen Auto Museum Foundation*

the dealers. The technically modern but unrefined K70 was not successful despite its water cooled front engine and front drive. Only the T2 held the flag high as a bestseller.

The main responsibility for this existence-threatening crisis was attributed to the VW leadership for its years of mismanagement. Nordhoff and his successor Kurt Lotz rested too long on the laurels of the Beetle and Transporter. Then, too, the high-volume models of the time were not really new developments, but just modified derivatives of the Beetle, whose day was nearing its end. Very fearful of losing further areas of the market, the Volkswagen management, led by the new chairman Rudolf Leiding, invested about a billion marks in the development of new models. Since time was flying, Audi, where the Audi 80 had been developed to production readiness under the leadership of Ludwig Kraus, had to help at first. The middle-class car from Ingolstadt was put on the market as of 1973 with added notchback and kombi variants as the "VW Passat." It replaced the obsolescent Type 3 after eleven years. The production of the barely younger Fridolin was also halted without a replacement, a further step was made to make Volkswagen a competitor again. But those in Wolfsburg had two more aces up their sleeves: the Scirocco and Golf models designed by Giugiaro. Shortly before their scheduled debut, the oil crisis shook the automotive world. This problem hit all manufacturers equally hard, but Volkswagen in particular. In the ranks of great German businesses, Volkswagen sank from first to seventh place, [p. 90] with a deficit of 800 billion marks! Amid this turbulence the Scirocco and Golf entered the international market in March and May 1974. Their design and concept generally gained great approval. For the time being, Volkswagen was saved.

"The VW Camping Wagon is a Volkswagen with which you are at home everywhere," said the advertising in the brochures of the time. "In the mountains it is your dwelling and shelter hut. In the solitude of the forests and lakes, your blockhouse. At the seashore, your private hotel." *Photo: Volkswagen Auto Museum Foundation*

In these tense times the Transporter was particularly in the spotlight. For one thing, it was the last gold-medalist of the Volkswagen firm, for another, at the 1972 Olympic Games in Munich, where, as satirists remarked, it was involved in more events than the athletes who competed for medals. In the Olympic year too, an automatic transmission was first made available. Of course, it was just for the larger engine and at a considerably higher price. Because of stricter American exhaust standards, the oil-bath air filter of the 1700 cc engine had to be replaced by a dry air filter. All models except the flatbeds also gained a battery protection panel for the starter battery, which was now turned 180 degrees to save space. [p. 91]

Other changes involved passive safety. The bumpers acquired new deformable elements. The completely reworked running gear passed the

Absolutely winter capable, even without four-wheel drive. Thanks to the rear engine, the Bulli had enough traction for difficult road conditions. *Photo: Volkswagen Auto Museum Foundation*

strict US test standards. With the introduction of safety bumpers, which were called "railroad rails" by the public, the earlier rubber-covered bumper step was dropped. A step set in behind the door now aided entry. In the cab, standard safety belts were added. There were also new controls for the heater, fan and windshield wipers. For better recognition in traffic, the front directional lights were moved upward from the bumper area to near the fresh air intakes. The rain gutter was also moved inward, which lessened the wind noise. In the middle of the model year, all models were fitted with a more powerful AC generator instead of the earlier ADC type.

Not only in Europe, but also in the USA, an important export land for the VW, the T2 with camper body and opening roof was very popular as motor homes. *Photo: Volkswagen Auto Museum Foundation*

In a way, the VW Bus was the grandfather of the present-day family van. *Photo: Volkswagen Auto Museum Foundation*

In 1973 Volkswagen also turned to electric power. The first project was a joint effort, a T2 Transporter developed with Bosch, Varta, and the RWE power producer. The gigantic lead battery that produced 23.8 kW per hour was located under the cargo space and powered a rear-mounted remote-control DC drum motor, which produced a steady 17 kW (23 HP). The power was transmitted to the rear wheels by a one-step gearbox. For short-time top performance, 33.5 kW (45 HP) and a maximum torque of 160 nM could be called on. Since the lead battery alone added 850 kg to the weight, the test vehicle weighed a total of 2.2 tons when empty. The range of the vehicle at 70 kph was 50 to 80 km, depending on how it was driven. For everyday use it was too little, but for material movement in big factories or as a mail truck, it was completely sufficient. Specially tied sales packages, which could be bought or leased with the vehicle, the battery and various servicing, found a surprisingly good reception in the economy. With the high base price of 42,595 DM (US $13,300), barely 70 electric Transporters were sold. The Tennessee Valley Authority, a power producer in the USA, bought ten of them – five box vans and five flatbeds – for a planned large-scale fleet test. On the initiative of the US Department of Energy, the first Volkswagen hybrid vehicle also appeared in 1973. The combustion engine of the T2 "City Taxi" bus drove an electric motor, mounted before the rear axle, via a hydrodynamic converter and an electropneumatic clutch. In purely electric driving, a maximum range of 40 km could be covered. In hybrid use, a consumption saving of some 15 could be achieved.

In August 1973, the obligatory model revision was comparatively unspectacular. The drum brakes were now self-adjusting and had vision holes in the brake plates, so that one could check the brake power from outside. In the Camper, the tipping joint for the opening roof moved from the pillar to the rear column. Changes to the locking system were somewhat more inclusive. The front doors were again secured with push buttons, the sliding door gained an automatic lock. The function of the unlocking lever was changed so that when the door was closed,

the lock was fully engaged at once. A fuel filler closed from outside replaced the earlier fuel flap. In the interior, a quartz clock with a second hand replaced the earlier impulse clock. For better light, a headlight washer system could be had for a price. The flat engine produced 68 HP from a displacement of 1795 cc. The maximum torque rose to 129 nM at 3000 rpm. The high fuel consumption, though, remained the same, which was to have unfavorable effects in time of oil boycotts and rising gasoline prices. While a car's fuel consumption had previously played a minor role, an armed conflict in the Near East inspired hasty rethinking.

In the fourth Israeli-Arab War of October 1973, the Arab states used oil as a weapon for the first time. An oil boycott was placed on the USA and the Netherlands for their pro-Israeli policy, and it had an effect on the other Western nations. The Organization of Petroleum Exporting Countries (OPEC), to which some non-Arabic producer nations also belonged, quadrupled the price of crude oil. The Western oil companies' desire for profit pushed the prices farther upward. The result was the first global oil crisis. The German government reacted with drastic limits on energy use and turned back to native fossil fuels like coal and natural gas. An order for four auto-free Sundays in November and December of 1973 was to be more symbolic of how the public could be shown their dependence on crude oil and its limited availability. The impact of rising fuel prices increased the dry for new, thrifty vehicles. The so-called gas guzzlers were suddenly unwanted. In 1974, the most important year in Volkswagen's struggle for survival, sales of the T2 also dropped alarmingly. While 65,168 of them had been sold in Germany in 1973, only 48,330 were sold in 1974. A year later the numbers fell even more seriously: despite large price cuts, only 46,910 new registrations were reported. Financial flexibility for the development of a new, thrifty engine was not to be had. The capital outlay for the Golf was too high. The purchase of a foreign diesel engine, as Opel had already done with the Peugeot self-igniter, was soon seen as impossible for the rear-engine concept of the Transporter.

On July 1, 1974 the last Beetle came off the assembly line in Wolfsburg. The stocks at the Emden and Brussels works were sufficient to meet its small demand in Europe. The production of the unfortunate Type 4 was also halted, but its engine lived on in the T2. In hopes of ease in the energy policy, the T2 was again upgraded. In the changed ignition setting, and the voltage regulator was integrated into the AC generator.

On February 10, 1975, Toni Schmücker took over the chair of the VW hierarchy from his unhealthy predecessor Leiding, who had used a strict economy program and the introduction of the new front-drive models to save the firm from

The successor in the form of the T3 already flitted through the automotive press when in 1978 VW put a special model called the "Silverfish" on the market. The Kombi with a flat roof and finished all in metallic silver gained interest with its extensive equipment, including dark blue velour seats, chromed bumpers, tinted glass, and a sliding roof. The luxury Transporter, of which some 1600 were sold, was powered by the 70 HP engine of the Type 4. *Photo: Volkswagen Auto Museum Foundation*

excitement of the world soccer championship victory in 1974, the seats were given a standard covering of imitation leather and passed more comfortably. The chrome strip formerly at belt-line height on the L models now formed a line with the door handles. Otherwise, the sliding door, reaching well into the roof of the high-roof transporter, was now given a practical locking system. The Box Van, like the Kombi a year later, was optionally available with added coil springs on the rear axle, which raised the load limit to 1.2 tons. The engine technology all remained as before, other than a

the disaster. Even though the crisis was not yet over, the signs pointed to expansion again: The VW LT was introduced as the second pillar of the Transporter realm, introducing important styling elements of the later T3. The small truck offered in three weight classes as LT 28, LT 31, and LT 35 had a [p. 95] front engine with rear drive and a rear axle with leaf springs. The LT was available as a box van, flatbed, or cab on a chassis. Only a year after its premiere it already held more than 30% of the market.

Since the T2 showed clear technical deficits in direct comparison, the development of the successor T3 model was approved on May 8, 1975. Though originally designed as a forward-looking small transporter, the capital was too small, so instead a thoroughly modernized T2 with a new body and more economical engines was on the agenda. Until that happened, changes were planned for the present model.

Regardless of the higher gasoline prices, the T2c was given more power as of August 1, 1975. The flat engine now developed a good 70 HP at 4200 rpm from a displacement of 1970 cc. The maximum torque was 140 nM at 2800 rpm. To put all the power on the road with as little loss as possible, the axle gear reduction was raised and the clutch diameter was enlarged to 228 mm. The automatic transmission, still optional, was also redeveloped. In place of the formerly used Type 003 with manual kickdown and vacuum control, the newly developed Type 010 automatic with rod burden indication, electric kickdown activation and laminated (instead of belt) brakes was introduced. For all engines, a connecting rod replaced the previous throttle cable, regardless the type of transmission. To save money, all the flatbeds were fitted with cast plastic lock housings at the rear and the hatch cover. On the dashboard there was, for the first time, a hand-brake warning light available for a price. Besides that, the dial of the speedometer was now completely backed in black for better legibility in sunlight.

The German Federal Republic faced a turning point in internal policy in 1975. With the abduction of the Berlin CDU Chairman Peter Lorenz on February 27, 1975, terrorists of the "June 2 Movement" demanded the release of four detained supporters of South Yemen. For the first time, the German government gave in to terrorist demands to protect human lives. [p. 96] On May 21, 1975, the Stammheim trials marked the beginning of the struggle with terrorists of the Red Army faction, which had created national tension since 1968. Two years later the wave of terror hit its brutal high point with the fatal attacks on three leading German officials and the skyjacking of the Lufthansa "Landshut" plane. Public life was as good as crippled, even though the situation was said to be firmly under control. Since the impact of the oil crisis were nowhere near being resolved, a new economic crisis spread. In its course, the weaknesses of the German economic structure were shown. Along with the especially hard-hit coastal regions, it was especially the Rhein-Ruhr district, the onetime leader of the Economic Miracle, that had to struggle with high unemployment and overcapacity.

In 1978, the VW Transporter was given off-road capability, which resulted in the first of five official test vehicles of the T2 type with switch-on front drive. With the four other vehicles, the first tests under real conditions were made the next winter. Lack of interest among possible customers like the Army or catastrophe protection caused the project to be halted. *Photo: Volkswagen Auto Museum Foundation*

In view of these developments, sales in the German auto industry dropped noticeably. The competition of Japanese cars on the German market caused further, unexpected reverses. While the Passat had to fight off the Japanese competition directly, the VW Transporter had it much easier. Since only Japanese car models were exported to Germany at first, the T2b remained safe, at first, from the Asiatic competition. Thus the sales figures remained at a comparatively high level to the end of its life cycle, with an average of 54,795 sales in Germany between 1976 and 1979.

While the T3 was already taking on its initial form in Wolfsburg in 1976, The T1 was still being built in Brazil. With over 66,000 vehicles sold, it was more successful than ever before. Yet there too, a model change was in the works. During the production year, the Brazilian T1 was given the front appearance of the T2b, ending Volkswagen's

Under Gustav Mayer's leadership, VW developed a prototype utility vehicle, though further development was vetoed by the management. The engineers later gained from the acquired experience in developing the T3 "Synchro." *Photo: Volkswagen Auto Museum Foundation*

this great production, the need for employees in the Hannover works was moving in the other direction. While 28,728 workers were employed in 1971, there were only 17,997 in 1977. The growing automation in the production process meant fewer employees, so a retirement regulation at 59 years was agreed on. The T2 also changed slowly into its old age. Upgrades for the 1978 model year were limited to a steering wheel that was easier to grip and had wider spokes, a more stable stopper on the front doors, and the dropping of the vent windows in the passenger space. Instead, the middle pane was now divided, and fitted with a slider for a price.

In its last production year, the T2 was fitted with automatic driver and passenger safety belts in August 1978. Much more interesting was the revival of a special edition with the "Special Model" designation of the Samba Bus. Made in a small series of 1600 vehicles, the "Bus L Eight-Seater Special Model" was put on the market. [p. 98] this luxury liner, painted metallic silver with a 70 HP engine, offered standard front headrests, a heatable rear windshield, a radio, rear vent windows, and a big steel roof. Seat upholstery, floor carpets, and inside coverings were done in an elegant medium blue. Although the special equipment package was clearly more reasonably priced than buying it all separately, the Special Model was no bargain. With a basic price of 19,495 DM (US $9400), the eight-seater known popularly as the "Silverfish" shared the price range of the upper-middle-class cars such as the Audi 100 or Opel Commodore at the end of the seventies.

era of the two-piece windshield after almost thirty years. Since its successor was already the focus in Germany, there were few changes made to the T2 in 1976. Beyond minor detail changes to the fuel pump, intake valves and drive belts, the front seats were multi-adjustable. In addition, the wall between the cab and passenger space was removed from some models.

In 1977, the 2,277,307th T2 was finished, making a total of four million VW Transporters. Despite

In September 2005, Volkswagen announced that air-cooled engine production would end with a special model, limited to 200 vehicles, of the Kombi Prata Series. The model, painted "Silver Light Metallic" with green windows and tinted windshield, was offered for 39,200 Brazilian reais (equaling some 17,300 Euros). *Photo: Volkswagen Auto Museum Foundation*

In 1978 the T2 became off-road capable. Under the leadership of its chairman Gustav Mayer, the VW-Commercial Vehicle Development department built the first prototypes of a T2 with switch-on front drive. Without the blessing of the firm's management, four more vehicles followed as "make-work measures" and had their first tests under real conditions in the winter of 1978-79. To prove the superior characteristics of the new system, Mayer even crossed the Sahara with the four-wheel-drive T2 a little later, and VW engineer Henning Duckstein was able to traverse the Grand Erg Oriental in Algeria, said to be impassable, in one.

Yet the market chances of an all-wheel-drive T2 were seen quite critically by the VW management. Besides little response from the public, there were no inquiries from potential large-scale buyers like the Bundeswehr or catastrophe protection services. Thus the all-wheel-drive development was halted. Only years later was the experience used in the design of the Audi Quattro and T3 "Synchro."

But the T2 was called on once more to test alternative drive technology. In 1978-79 more than 150 were rebuilt as electric vehicles and fitted with various energy storing systems. The results, though, were worse than expected. The last curtain finally fell in Germany in July 1979. The demise of the T2 left the assembly line at the Hannover works open for its successor, the T3. In Brazil, though, it was still produced as the T2c as of 1997. It was again air-cooled, but with a squarer roof shape, As one of the cheapest vehicles in South America, it lacked modern features such as servo steering, air bags, or central locking. Even a heater, because of the tropical climate, [p. 99] was not made standard. The 1600 cc boxer engine had lower compression because of the very widely variations in fuel quality, and it produced 58 HP at 4200 rpm. Yet it moved the 1250 kg rear-drive vehicle from zero to 100 kph in 58.9 seconds. Volkswagen of Brazil optimistically listed its top speed at 120 kph. The T2c was available as a Kombi, box van, and bus. Production figures remain constant at 40 vehicles per day. In December 2005, with the silver "Prata" special model, the last air-cooled T2c left the factory. Its successor, the similar-looking "T2 Kombi," was introduced in January 2006 with only one available body style. At the heart of the eight-seater is an 80 HP "Total flex" boxer engine with 1390 cc displacement, a regulated catalytic converter, and electric fuel injection. Set up for the regional conditions, the enginer, supposedly "innovation of Brazil," can be run on any mixture of gasoline and alcohol. The water-cooled T2 is recognizable by its black plastic radiator grille, which gives the Brazilian Transporter, available only in white, a rather unusual appearance.

While the T2 still runs on the rough roads and streets of South America every day, it and, particularly, its forerunner, theT1, have meanwhile become rarities in Germany, along with the VW 1500 or Mercedes /8 built in much smaller numbers. The high use value, compared to a modern large sedan, is another positive side effect, and is often "the" argument in favor of persuading one's better half to buy such a versatile "oldie." But the general interest in the VW bus as a cult object also has its negative side. For rare models in particular, the prices have

meanwhile risen into the stratosphere. While a very well-kept T1 Samba bus could be had ten years ago for the equivalent of 10,000 to 15,000 Euro (US $5200-7500), the panoramic buses have long since passed the 50,000 Euros (US $65,000) boundary today. Even for an ordinary T1 box van, more than 20,000 Euros (US $26,000) will be paid today. It is a rising trend! And this happens even though its "use value" is surely the motivation for only a very few of the people who buy it. But when the VW fan has been infected with the Bulli fever, utilitarian vehicles are also of interest, and the high price for the coal truck of his childhood or the milk truck of his student job is no longer a hindrance. It is similar with the T2, where more than 20,000 Euros (US $26,000) are paid for rare L models like the "Clipper" or "Silverfish." Campers are also in demand as never before and thus go for the highest prices now. Yet we might wish that the Volkswagen Transporter would remain affordable for all those for whom it was once developed: the people.

The generations meet: As the successor to the T2, Volkswagen introduced the T3 in 1979. Even though the T3 models are still active in daily use today to some extent, they are rarely seen on the street. For a long time, examples of this series gained popularity as the last representatives of the rear-engine generation. The early models have even attained "Oldtimer" status already. *Photo: Volkswagen Auto Museum Foundation*

Above: The "Clipper," introduced in 1967 as the successor to the Samba Bus, was to make the T2 interesting to normal car customers as well. The steel roof, two-tone paint, and chrome trim were standard, but the left sliding door of the L-Bus shown here cost extra. *Photo: Jörg Hajt*

Opposite page, above: Somewhat unusual for a luxury bus was its original use as a commercial vehicle for a haberdasher, who did without the middle seat. It was added to this Clipper by the present owner in the process of restoration. *Photo: Jörg Hajt*

Opposite page, below: When this luxury bus was made in 1969, Volkswagen had to give up the copyrighted model name, "Clipper." Yet the nautical nickname remained in VW circles for the top model, now called "Eight-Seater L" or "Seven-Seater L". *Photo: Jörg Hajt*

A perfectly maintained T2a of the now very rare 1972 model year is this Type 24 Eight-seat L, which, because its modifications anticipated the T2b, was also called the "Zwitterbus." *Photo: Jörg Hajt*

The most visible differences from the "old" T2a were, as of August 1970, the rear fender ridges, the rectangular taillights and the flatter engine hood. The gas filler also finally moved outside the area of the sliding door. *Photo: Jörg Hajt*

Box vans like this T2a of the Modelia dress shop in Oldenburg typified the scene on German streets until well into the 1980s. *Photo: Jörg Hajt*

This former builder's van from the Esser KG firm is a 1970 T2a box van put back into its original condition. It reached its present owner after having served as a fire truck. *Photo: Alexander Prinz*

While the VW Transporter was commonly used for rescue service, it played only a small role in the funeral business. This unrestored T2a Type 2110 was put into service by the town of Rohrbach by Wiener Neustadt in 1968, and is one of the very few existing VW hearses. *Photo: Jörg Hajt*

On account of the rear engine, the coffin had to be loaded rather high, which is why very few undertakers chose the reliability of the VW box van. *Photo: Jörg Hajt*

This T2b TSF box van made in 1974 was rebuilt as a historic service truck of the Düsseldorf Rheinbahn. The vehicle belonged to the professional firefighters of Düsseldorf until 2004 and was used by them in preventive fire protection. *Photo: Jörg Hajt*

Only since its restoration in 2006 has the ex-TSF with Ziegler body borne the logo of the historic Linie D work group and the orange warning color of the Rheinbahn service fleet. *Photo: Jörg Hajt*

As a practical combination of "youngtimer" and useful vehicle, this T2b is still used by its owner for many transport tasks. *Photo: Jörg Hajt*

In November 1979 this new Type 2110 box van was of the very last T2s built in Germany. Large price reductions made the T2b interesting for businesses even after the T3 appeared. It was completely restored in 2006. *Photo: Jörg Hajt*

Above: This unevenly heavily burdened T2a box van is also in daily use by a spare-parts dealer, but has not been scrapped after more than 40 years. A special feature of a former bakery van is its additional left sliding door. *Photo: Jörg Hajt*

Left: The cargo space of the box van still offers enough room for the most varied transport tasks by today's standards. The T2 was not very common without a back window, as in this vehicle. *Photo: Jörg Hajt*

Unrestored and with the typical patina is this T2b double-cab Type 2650 put into service by the Army, and used today as a transport van in everyday civilian life. *Photo: Jörg Hajt*

Rear view of the military double-cab truck. Note the windows in the tailgate—called "loopholes" in army jargon. *Photo: Jörg Hajt*

As a municipal vehicle this large-space wooden covered truck was built in 1970. Between 1990 and 2006 it was unused, then restored carefully for more than 20,000 Euros (US $13,700), and now serves its new home town of Fladungen by following an old tradition as an information truck for church news. *Photo: Stefan Gross*

With a cargo space of 5.20 square meters, this large rear body has a definite advantage in space over the standard rear body. As was customary with all such trucks, it could also be had with a locking vault under the rear deck. *Photo: Stefan Gross*

A real rarity among light dump trucks is this large-area wooden-bodied Type 2611c with mechanical-hydraulic tipping mechanism. The vehicle, built by Westfalia in 1976, was still in everyday use until a few years ago and is still in its unrestored original condition. *Photo: Jörg Hajt*

As elegant as it is rustic, this "Whisky Transporter" is a Type 2610 open truck of the last series. The wooden walls were made for the restoration and show that it is not only vehicles in original form that can look right. *Photo: Tom Aebersold*

Above: For combined transport and medical service, the Red Cross group in Söhlde bought this 2312 Kombi in 1973 as a "personnel transport wagon with auxiliary patient carrier." The vehicle is seen here with a Red Cross medical trailer of the Ernst Hahn firm in Fellbach. *Photo: Jörg Hajt*

Opposite page: This 1978 Kombi Type 2316 was used by the Readiness Police in Hamburg. Equipped with a sound set made by the Bögel firm of Bückeburg, the vehicle was used as a loudspeaker truck at major events and dangerous situations. *Photo: Jörg Hajt*

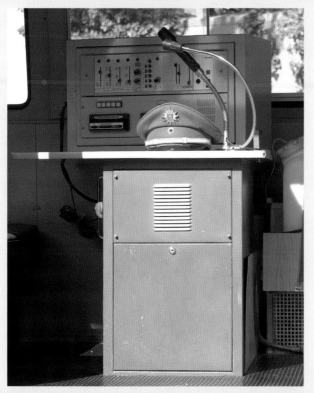

Left: A look inside the bus shows the control center of the sound system looking old-fashioned by today's standards. Photo: Jörg Hajt

In rural areas in particular, the universal utility of the personnel transport proved to be a great advantage. Even if the makeshift patient carrier allowed no medical treatment, patients could be transported with it. *Photo: Jörg Hajt*

Revised as a camper, this KTW Type 2710 of April 1972 was in service with the Buderus works fire company until 1998. The unrestored vehicle is one of only 1600 "Zwitter-KTWs" that were built, and serves its present owner as a camping bus. *Photo: Jörg Hajt*

Firefighting specialists Ziegler produced this T2b Type 2111 TSF fire truck used by the volunteer firefighters of Dommershausen, which normally had a higher-set front bumper to increase the slope angle. *Photo: Jörg Hajt*

After the catastrophe protection units were disbanded, the city firefighters took over many of their vehicles, including this T2b command van, which is still in service with the Gladbeck volunteer firefighters. *Photo: Georg Wattsche*

This T2b Type 2111c TSF-T was delivered to the Cordima fire company in December 1972. The vehicle still has its original firefighting equipment, including a pump operated by a VW industrial motor.

After thirty years' service, 13,000 kilometers and only two documented uses at fires, this perfectly maintained, unrestored factory fire truck was mustered out in 2002. *Photo: Jörg Hajt*

These two splendidly maintained TSF-T simulate emergency action in this picture. At left is a 1971 T2a, which, after being used at the 1972 Olympic Games, went into service with the Rolfsbüttel firefighters. At right is a T2a of 1969 that earned its bread with the Odisheim firefighters until 1997. *Photo: Jörg Hajt*

This T2a Type SO 62 Camping Wagon, built by Westfalia of Wiedenbrück in 1968 and precisely restored, shows the small raising roof that is seldom-seen today. *Photo: Klaus Jacklen*

The Westfalia raising roof also cuts a fine figured when closed. Thanks to the luggage rack that fits elegantly into the roof lines, the vehicle definitely looks more harmonious. *Photo: Jörg Hajt*

The Westfalia raising roof first displayed at the 1973 IAA, with a front luggage hatch and sloping roof silhouette gave the T2b Type 2319 Camping Wagon a very new feeling of spaciousness. *Photo: Jörg Hajt*

Typical of the SO 73/7 "Helsinki" equipment available since August 1974 were the colorful cloth seat covers and the typical furnishings in "spruce tones." *Photo: Jörg Hajt*

With the Type 2211 "Bus L Eight-Seater Special Model" introduced in 1978, VW offered for the first time a limited small series of 1600 Transporters. Because of the metallic silver paint, this luxury bus was popularly nicknamed the "Silverfish." *Photo: Jörg Hajt*

This special model, available only with the 70 HP engine (note the exhaust pipe on the right side), had standard front head rests, a defroster for the back window, a radio, rear vent windows, and a big steel roof. The interior décor was an elegant medium blue. *Photo: Jörg Hajt*

This photo shows a 1977 double-cab Type 2650 from the fleet of the Hannover city government. Now restored, it pulls a Wolperding SO 14 trailer on 1969. *Photo: Jörg Hajt*

As with the T1, the T2 SO 14 long-load carrier only had a simple pair of posts to hold long items. To haul tools on his trailer one needed to turn to the more expensive SO 24 with a hanger. *Photo: Jörg Hajt*

The Brazilian Special Model "Prata" bus, like the "Silverfish" in Germany, was the high point and end of the air-cooled T2c era. *Photo: Jörg Hajt*

On demand, the "Prata" could also be imported in a sporting version with black-tinted glass and special wheels with wider tires. The air-cooled boxer engine, producing 56 HP, remained unchanged. *Photo: Jörg Hajt*

Forty of these air-cooled T2c vans, built in Brazil until December 2005, found their way to Germany in 2006. Rather than chrome, plastic dominated them. The picture shows the two-seat box van in its typical Brazilian form. *Photo: Jörg Hajt*

Since 2006, the present-day Brazilian Transporter, now called Series "T2 Kombi," has been built with an 80 HP water-cooled 1.4 liter "TotalFlex Engine" that runs on gasoline and/or alcohol. The South American van, available only in white, is characterized by its black plastic grille. *Photo: Jörg Hajt*

A new dream car for the nostalgic: a rebuilt luxury version of the T2c with leather upholstery, chrome trim, and different roof structure. The two-tone finish could be had for all imported Brazilian vehicles for an extra 1800 Euros (US $2100).
*Photo: Archives*

# BUYING ADVICE

There are only a few classic vehicles that, at an advanced age, have as high a useful value as the Volkswagen Transporter. This leads to the fact that both the T1 and T2 have enjoyed growing popularity and increasing value in the last few years. What is a good value for their owners, though, conceals many dangers for the potential buyer. After all, not all vehicles on the auto market were perfectly maintained. Many vehicles are real "blinders" that, with lacking care, can soon turn into incalculable money pits. With all the excitement about the Transporter, a purchase should therefore always be made with the necessary emotional detachment, and the heart should be listened to only in the restoration or care of the vehicle. Whether a potential purchase is worth the requested price, often amounting to 10,000 Euros (US$13,000)or more, cannot always be determined at first glance. Thus a systematic analysis of the general condition is urgently advised.

To begin with, there should be a warning that not every T1 or T2 is necessarily worth buying, and that if one has doubts, one does best to turn the "rare collector's item," as the seller calls it, over to an appraiser, instead of wanting to awaken an auto held together only by patches to a new life. Here, as a rule, the unwelded but presumably more heavily rusted-out auto proves to be the more forgettable restoration object. This applies to both the T1 and its successor, the T2. Even if the problem areas of the two vehicles are the same at first glance, there are big differences to consider in evaluating them.

## Body and Bottom

As with all historic vehicles, the T1 and T2 were scarcely considered to be worth a lasting rust prevention. Thus massive damage to the whole body can be caused by rust. In a first inspection, the condition of the rubber window mouldings can be a first criterion for appraisal: If the rubber sticks out from the underside of the window frame or if bubbles of rust are seen in this area, one can presume with near-certainty that the vehicle's body and/or parts of the bottom are rusted through. In the front end, rainwater penetrates far behind the bumpers if the seals are not good, so that massive rust damage can occur

Vital for a perfect restoration is a fully uncovered body box. *Photo: Claus Missing*

there. The adjoining bottom panels under the doors are usually damaged inside and outside as well. Another weak point is the front wheel wells. In their upper parts, where they follow the entry steps, they almost always rust through, so that in a normal case masses of putty and/or patches are found. In the T2 as of the production month of August1970, the rust occurring in these areas, on account of the projecting wheel spindles, is especially heavy, and repairs are correspondingly expensive. In vehicles with seat belts, it also pays to look at the anchor points of the belts near the seats. Since a reinforcing panel was set in under the belt attachment bolt, [p. 127] the whole attachment often rusts, due to water getting between the two plates. Next one should examine the front floor space closely. Under the rubber mat, as a rule, the bottom panel has been attacked by rust and dirt buildup. At the transition from the floor to the wheel well, there are frequently small rusted-through spots as well. Here too, the longitudinal frame members with the lateral

extensions run to the front of the vehicle, and because of their angled and layered forms, these can be places of origin for rusting through to the interior. An intensive look at the inside bottom cannot hurt either. The rippled bottom panel often shows lines of rust. Dampness and street dirt often are collected by the transverse members running through this area, so that massive rusting here cannot be treated except by replacing the entire bottom including the small transverse members. Various dents in the big longitudinal members also give indication of their being rusted through, which can amount, in the worst case, to the complete instability of the entire body.

In flatbed trucks, the condition of the bed and the sidewalls should be examined critically. Small rust holes here are much less problematic than bent panels or wooden planks, which are also not so easy to find replacements for. For bodies with canvas tops, the hoops and their attachments should be checked for a secure hold and rust damage. In addition, the back wall of the cab is a problem zone for all flatbed trucks. Especially on the transition from the bed to the cab, rust damage is common and can eat its way into the interior. So make sure to look behind the seats. Another problem area is the storage cabinet under the bed on the passenger side. Besides defects to the locking mechanism, the closed area favors rust and mold. But be careful: replacements for the box called the "treasure chest" by many Bulli drivers are very hard top find, so they should be repaired if possible. This is also true of the

mechanics and hydraulics of tipping beds. It is obvious that firmly attached trailer hitches can also rust; after that we can go on to examine the general evaluation of the vehicle.

The inside and outside front steps are a danger zone in all Transporters. Here one should absolutely search for possible rust spots, armed with a screwdriver and flashlight. Replacement pieces have been available for a long time, but there is strong rust damage in this area resulting from incorrect replacement and rust treatment. In the T1 with hinged doors, rusting through at the doorstep level is, fortunately, somewhat less common, but never to be ruled out because of the vehicle's age. In vehicles with sliding doors, the outside threshold area must also be examined very closely. Beyond that, there is danger of rust damage and impaired sliding ability to be checked for in the entire sliding mechanism. One should also save some time for a look at the interiors of all doors. It is advisable to remove all the interior coverings. A seller with honest intentions should surely understand this. The front doors of all models are regarded as faulty designs, as they consist, in part, of up to four layers of sheet metal. In the interstices moisture and dirt settle in the course of time, making an ideal location for all kinds of rusting. The lower door edges, in particular, are victims of rust in almost all vehicles, and though they often are unskillfully repaired. The middle doors also suffer from rust on their bottom edges, since the rain water that gets inside very often settles there.

The windshield edges are among the very weakest points. There is usually damage along the lower edges. *Photo: Claus Missing*

The attachment points of the front seats and the angle of the interior panel and the door frame tend to develop holes. *Photo: Claus Missing*

The outside door sills should be examined very critically. If there is rust here, it will be very expensive to deal with. *Photo: Claus Missing*

Almost all Transporters begin to rust in the spray area. If it looks as bad as it does here, it can no longer be repaired by simple patches. *Photo: Claus Missing*

Under the front rubber mat, the bottom panel is often rusty. The transition from the pedal floor to the wheel well is also very prone to rust damage. *Photo: Claus Missing*

Rainwater dripping in from above is the reason for the rust damage in the area of the bumper attachments of almost all models. *Photo: Claus Missing*

The rippled bottom panel in the cargo space often shows lines of rust holes. If the transverse members are also rusted, the situation is serious. *Photo: Claus Missing*

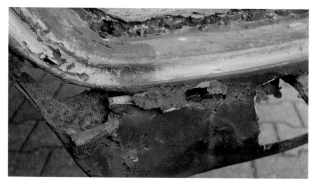

Nothing works any more: The curved plates under the doors are among the most rust-prone components of the front of the vehicle. *Photo: Claus Missing*

A bad point in the worst sense of the word is the jack insertion point, where the damage looks about like this on all restoration projects. *Photo: Claus Missing*

Look at the bottom of the vehicle: Wherever frame members and panels meet in more than one layer, poor rust treatment can result in problems. *Photo: Claus Missing*

In vehicles with sliding doors, the covering of the sliding rail is susceptible to dirt and rust. The joint of the sliding mechanism is also likely to have wear and thus breakage as it gets older!

Go on to the rear wheel wells. The rear ends of the outside ridges before the wheel cutout are extremely threatened by rust in all Transporters. The same is true of the entire spray area, where grit, salt, and mud largely settle, and not only

because of poor maintenance. In the T2 with wide rear wheel arches (since August 1970), these could rust through on their whole length, since they were made double-walled. In this case the whole wheel arch must be replaced. The area under the taillights also develops rust easily and should also be checked. Likewise the engine and rear hatches. In the older models, the inner frame is usually more heavily involved than the outer panel. In the T2, curiously, it is often the other way around. In the engine compartment, the attachment panel by the starter battery has been a problem area. Water splashed from below and leaking battery acid from above affect every panel. The fixed rear panel behind the rear bumper also tends to disintegrate, especially when the vehicle has been driven for a long time with a defective exhaust system and the metal has been overheated. In the T2b, the longitudinal members to the left and right of the engine cause trouble, making repairs to the inner frame with an installed engine very difficult. In models built after the August 1971 production month, it is also worth taking a look at the added members and braces.

On the bottom, the T1 in particular begins to rust at the jack insertion point. But the T2 should be checked here too. These areas may have been patched one or more times even in well-kept vehicles. As a rule, they rust through at their outer end, where the reinforcing bar is inserted. The inside thresholds extend behind the front jack points. They are also extremely likely to rust in all models. Between the jack point and the two longitudinal members, the condition of the front transverse member, through which the heating duct passes, should also be checked. This almost always falls victim to rust in the T1 and T2—as does the heating duct itself in all models. A tip: The heating duct should be wrapped as much as possible when repairs are made and it is reused, for an unprotected heating duct makes the heat supplied to the interior diminish noticeably. As a rule, the T2b usually has a plastic tube, so that this problem does not occur in that model. In the T1 and T2a, the rear transverse member also tends to rust; in the T2b, the duct to which the rear spring rods are attached can rust completely through. The outer components such as the bumpers, handles and mirrors very often look much better than [p. 130] their condition actually is. Here one should also seek out weak points carefully, even though most such parts are very easy to buy.

# Powerplant and Running Gear

Now let us look at the engine. Even if only power aggregates from Kafer & Co., which have been tested millions of times, have been installed, this does not necessarily guarantee their proverbial longevity. The limited horsepower never had an easy time moving the comparatively heavy buses and Transporters, so the engines were driven too often at full throttle. This meant that many engines had to battle bad sealing and excessive wear caused by high temperatures. The oil cooler in the blower box, the gasket tappet seals, and the seal ring behind the clutch were especially affected.

known for their longevity, replacement should be done in any case.

The gearbox from the Beetle proves to be troublesome, usually caused by rough use of the shift lever. Often the reverse lock is also defective. Then the bearing box of the forward shift rod is usually damaged. To replace it, the engine and gearbox have to be removed! If shifting is especially difficult in cold weather, changing the gearbox oil usually helps. Many Bulli drivers swear by modern gearbox oil from Castrol. Every owner must decide for himself whether this really helps.

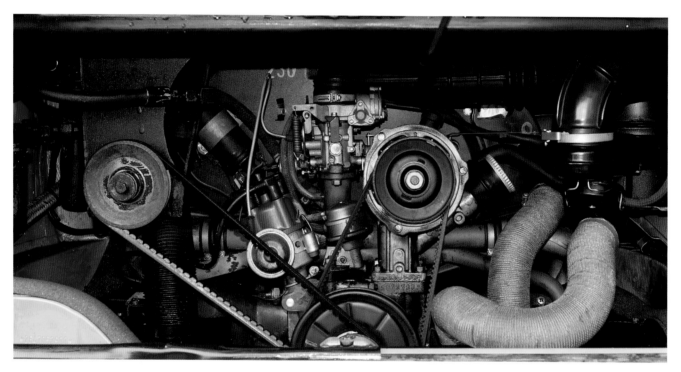

A good look into the engine space, as in this T2b flatbed with standard engine and added cherry-picker drive, should always be part of an inspection. In case of visible oil loss, extreme caution is advised.

The carburetor, on the other hand, was very robust and gave little reason to complain. The throttle flap shafts, however, should be checked for excessive play and overall functioning. Please note that in the last production year the incoming air warming was changed. Until then it was taken in on the underside of the cylinder head; as of May 1966 this was done by a heat exchanger. Heat exchangers often show rust on the groove in the middle of the housing and the pipe passages to the muffler. Danger: with faulty sealing, exhaust can get into the interior! If it is an original VW heat exchanger, repairs of small holes are worth making. With heat exchangers from the parts trade, which are not

But the four-speed box is not prone to lose oil. As a rule, the oil goes up the front of the box at the entry of the shift lever. Oil loss from a defective seal ring in the clutch housing is thus rare.

The engine and gearbox weaknesses generally apply to the T2 as well. The automatic transmission available with the Type 4 engine, though, has proved to be very reliable, but needs regular oil changes.

Because of their comparatively meager engine power, even the 47 and 50 HP engines may have wear, caused by high engine speeds, at the aforementioned places. Their hot overworking can often cause cracks in the cylinder heads between the spark plugs and valve seats, but the thermally stressed engines also blow out on the gasket surfaces between the cylinder heads and the cylinders. The "hear-see test" has proved itself as a practical test here: if a more or less strong hissing sound is heard while the engine is idling, and if the spark-plug caps are strongly blackened, crack damage is fairly certain. To be completely sure, of course, remove the cylinder head. Atomizing the fuel mixture can also be troublesome, especially in the 50 HP version. The throttle flap bar of the Solex downdraft carburetor is often damaged and the idle vents are loose because of stripped threads. If a carburetor is defective, it can generally be overhauled only in special workshops that can refurbish the throttle flap boxes. A good used carburetor is sometimes the best alternative. It is vital to obtain the identical type with the correct number of jets. If all goes well, the 50 HP engine of the T1 is the better choice for everyday use, for it does not have to run constantly under high pressure.

The next step is checking the axial play of the crankshaft. If the belt pulley can be moved back and forth visibly, caution is urged. Too much axial play does not necessarily mean the end for the engine! In a removed engine, though, it can be adjusted anew.

Real driving pleasure, though, comes only with the flat engine introduced in August 1971. The 66 HP, 1700 cc powerplant of the VW 411 (Type 4) obviously has less trouble with the vehicle's weight, so that most flat engines are in a low-wear condition. Pistons and cylinder (heads) generally last as long as the engine does. Totals of 150,000 km and more, with good maintenance, are not a rarity; cracks between spark plugs and valve seats are the only exception. Now and then cracks form in the outlet channels. Then the valve seats can loosen or the valves can "eat into" the seats. If replacement is needed, complete Type 4 engines and their parts, are definitely more costly, for, among other things, they are less common and are often used for high-powered Beetle tuning. The later 1800 and 2000 cc engines in particular, producing 68 and 70 HP, are especially expensive. The Achilles heel of the Type 4 engines, though,

is not their price, but their suitability for running a bus. For example, not only is the fuel pump installed near the clutch exposed directly to road dirt, it is also extremely hard to get at. Also, the heat flaps are mounted separately in two housings on the ducts of the heat exchanger, where they must always be subjected to wind and weather. As with the 1600, a look into the flat engine's two carburetors should not be omitted. Do the throttle flap rods have too much play? Do the idle switch vents sit properly? Are the vacuum and equalizing systems sealed. Note: If the engine draws "wrong" air, it can overheat from too thin a mixture. The result would be serious engine damage. Included in the buying decision should be the considerably higher fuel consumption of the Type 4 engine. While the standard engine uses about 11 liters in 100 km, the top-of-the-line engine uses three or four liters more. For all engines, always check the oil. Very black or dirty motor oil indicates much engine wear or bad seals. Too low or extremely varying oil pressure, on the other hand, results from a defective oil pump or worn bearings. If the engine runs rough or unevenly, it is the bearings; if the oil pressure light goes off late or not at all, in eight out of ten cases it is the oil pump. Also necessary for any T1 and T2 is a critical look at the brakes. The very poorly dimensioned brake system inclines to uneven drums and swollen brake lines in all models. The brake discs (since 1971) are also often badly worn. A T2 used mainly as a utility vehicle often turns out to be in a condition that causes concern.

# Electrical Components

The electrical components of the T1 and T2 have proved to be reliable and trouble-free for their age. This applies to both the simple 6-volt system and the 12-volt system introduced in August 1966. If an electric problem does appear unexpectedly, the illogically arranged wiring unfortunately tries one's patience. In addition, many cable trees were [p. 132] damaged by unqualified amateurs, so that in such a case only a new cable can help. Normal electric troubles such as the failure of the directionals or taillights because of a bad contact can be cured as quickly as the replacement of a dead bulb. The light and signal system is itself a weak point in all series. For one thing, the switch

The dashboard of the first Bulli generation looks quite Spartan. Original gauges and steering wheels are now very rare and thus comparatively expensive to obtain.

One problem area at the front of the T2 is the rim attachments of the headlights. If the rust here is too bad, only the building of a new front panel will help.

Because of the design, the transition from the front directional light to the air intake of the T2b is a dust collector. If the vehicle was poorly maintained, rust is a danger in this area!

is often very loose or no longer installed correctly (in models to August 1972); for another, corrosion on the relays causes incorrect blinker rhythms, non-working high beams, or erratically working headlights or horns again and again. As a rule, the relays must be replaced. Here too, the safety boxes in which all the relays were housed as of 1969 should be sealed anew. If the load warning light glows softly or no longer goes out, it has usually "wiped out" the regulator of the generator. The generator itself is reliable in all models and is thus rarely a source of trouble.

# Obtaining Spare Parts

As long as obtaining spare parts refers to mechanical parts, there are scarcely any large problem areas for the T1 and T2. Many parts are identical to those of the Beetle and the engines of the T2 came from the Type 4. It is more of a problem to get body parts. Replacement panels for the T1 and T2a/b "Zwittermodell" are not always found quickly. For the interior, too, for some time not every part has been available. The obligatory trip to the auto recycler of a few years ago scarcely bears fruit now, because even a T2b has disappeared from the everyday street scene too long ago. Fortunately, there are numerous spare-parts dealers who have specialized in selling rare old vehicle parts. A look in a car magazine like *Oldtimer Markt* or contact with the nearest Bulli club can also be helpful in obtaining spare parts.

# TECHNICAL DATA

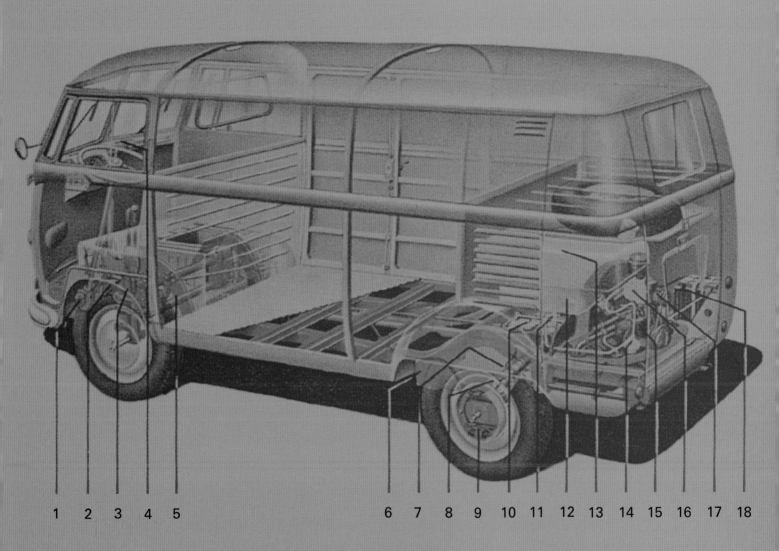

1 Steering gear
2 Brake master cylinder
3 Front shock absorber
4 Defroster vent
5 Front axle

6 Torsion bar mounting
7 Rear axle
8 Spur reduction gearing
9 Brake wheel cylinder
10 Gearbox
13 Fuel tank
14 Fuel pump

15 Distributor
16 Carburetor
17 Generator
18 Battery

# Technical Data of the T1 Transporter

| | 1100 | 1200 | 1200 | 1500 | 1500 |
|---|---|---|---|---|---|
| Engine | four-cylinder boxer engine | | | | |
| Displacement | 1131 cc | 1192 cc | | 1493 cc | |
| Bore x stroke | 75 x 64 mm | 77 x 64 mm | | 83 x 69 mm | |
| Power | 18.4 kW | 22 kW | 25 kW | 30.9 kW | 32.3 kW |
| HP at rpm | 25/3300 | 30/3400 | 34/3600 | 42/3800 | 44/4000 |
| Drive | rear wheel, reduced | | | | |
| Fuel mixing | 1 Solex downdraft carburetor | | | | |
| Valve operation | pushrods and rockers, central camshaft, driven by spur gear | | | | |
| Engine cooling | air-cooling with fan | | | | |
| Transmission | manual four-speed gearbox | | | | |
| Front suspension | crank link axle with bolts, 2 transverse spring rods | | | | |
| Rear suspension | Swing axle, longitudinal links, transverse spring rods | | | | |
| Brake system | hydraulic front and rear drum brakes | | | | |
| Length x width x height | 4190 x 1725 x 1940 mm (box van) | | | | |
| Wheelbase | 2400 mm (box van) | | | | |
| Body structure | Self-bearing all-steel with longitudinal and transverse members | | | | |
| Empty weight | 990 kg (box van with driver) | | | | |
| Top speed | 85 kph | 90 kph | 95 kph | 105 kph | 110 kph |

# TECHNICAL DATA

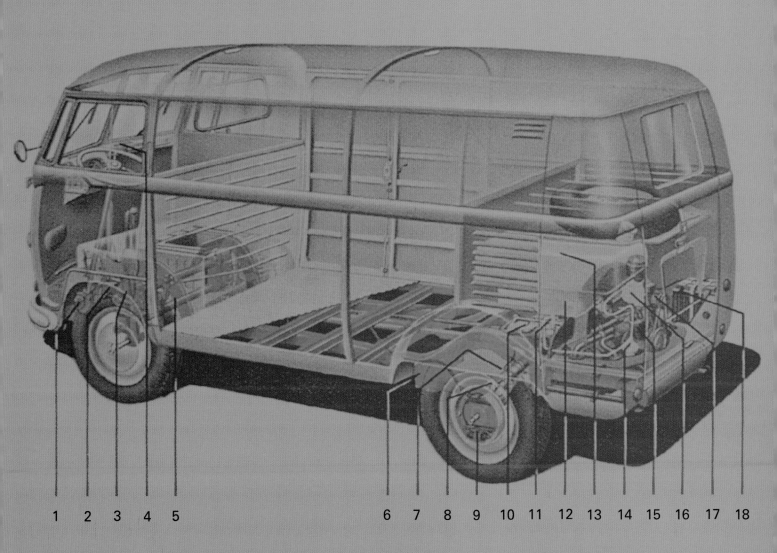

1    2    3    4    5          6   7   8   9   10   11   12   13   14   15   16   17   18

| | | |
|---|---|---|
| 1 Steering gear | 6 Torsion bar mounting | 15 Distributor |
| 2 Brake master cylinder | 7 Rear axle | 16 Carburetor |
| 3 Front shock absorber | 8 Spur reduction gearing | 17 Generator |
| 4 Defroster vent | 9 Brake wheel cylinder | 18 Battery |
| 5 Front axle | 10 Gearbox | |
| | 13 Fuel tank | |
| | 14 Fuel pump | |

# Technical Data of the T1 Transporter

| | 1100 | 1200 | 1200 | 1500 | 1500 |
|---|---|---|---|---|---|
| Engine | four-cylinder boxer engine | | | | |
| Displacement | 1131 cc | 1192 cc | | 1493 cc | |
| Bore x stroke | 75 x 64 mm | 77 x 64 mm | | 83 x 69 mm | |
| Power | 18.4 kW | 22 kW | 25 kW | 30.9 kW | 32.3 kW |
| HP at rpm | 25/3300 | 30/3400 | 34/3600 | 42/3800 | 44/4000 |
| Drive | rear wheel, reduced | | | | |
| Fuel mixing | 1 Solex downdraft carburetor | | | | |
| Valve operation | pushrods and rockers, central camshaft, driven by spur gear | | | | |
| Engine cooling | air-cooling with fan | | | | |
| Transmission | manual four-speed gearbox | | | | |
| Front suspension | crank link axle with bolts, 2 transverse spring rods | | | | |
| Rear suspension | Swing axle, longitudinal links, transverse spring rods | | | | |
| Brake system | hydraulic front and rear drum brakes | | | | |
| Length x width x height | 4190 x 1725 x 1940 mm (box van) | | | | |
| Wheelbase | 2400 mm (box van) | | | | |
| Body structure | Self-bearing all-steel with longitudinal and transverse members | | | | |
| Empty weight | 990 kg (box van with driver) | | | | |
| Top speed | 85 kph | 90 kph | 95 kph | 105 kph | 110 kph |

# Technical Data of the T2 Transporter

| | 1600 | 1600 | 1700 | 1800 | 2000 |
|---|---|---|---|---|---|
| Engine | four-cylinder boxer engine | | | | |
| Displacement | 1584 cc | | 1679 cc | 1795 cc | 1970 cc |
| Bore x stroke | 55 x 69 mm | | 90 x 66 mm | 93 x 66 mm | 94 x 71 mm |
| Power | 34.6 kW | 36.8 kW | 48.5 kW | 50 kW | 51.5 kW |
| HP at rpm | 47/4000 | 50/4000 | 66/4800 | 68/4200 | 70/4200 |
| Drive | rear wheel drive | | | | |
| Fuel mixing | 1 Solex downdraft carburetor | | 2 Solex downdraft carburetors | | |
| Valve operation | pushrods and rockers, central camshaft driven by spur gear | | | | |
| Engine cooling | air-cooling with fan | | | | |
| Transmission | manual four-speed | | manual 4-speed, optional/automatic 3-speed | | |
| Front suspension | single-wheel with double crank links, transverse rods | | | | |
| Rear suspension | transverse-link rear axle, transverse rods | | | | |
| Brake system | hydraulic front disc and rear drum brakes | | | | |
| Length x width x height | 4420 x 1765 x 1955 mm (box van) | | | | |
| Wheelbase | 2400 mm (box van) | | | | |
| Body structure | self-bearing all-steel with longitudinal and transverse members | | | | |
| Empty weight | 1175 kg (box van with driver) | | | | |
| Top speed | 105 kph | 110 kph | 125 kph | 127 kph | 127 kph |

# Bibliography

Michael Steinke, *Typenkompass VW Bus/Transporter 1949-1979*, Stuttgart 2003
Stefan Doliwa, *VW Transporter—Die technische Dokumentation*, Stuttgart 2000
Peter Kurze, *VW Bulli—Flotter Transporter*, Bielefeld 2010
Helmut M. Müller, *Schlaglichter der deutschen Geschichte*, Bonn 1990
Various information from periodicals such as *Oldtimer Markt, Motor Klassik*, etc.